A PERSONAL NARRATIVE OF A VISIT TO GHUZNI, KABUL AND AFGHANISTAN AND OF A RESIDENCE AT THE COURT OF DOST MOHAMED

WITH NOTICES OF RUNJIT SING, KHIVA AND THE RUSSIAN EXPEDITION

DOST MOHAMED KHAN.

London. Published by Whittaker and C° Ave-Maria Lane

A PERSONAL NARRATIVE
OF A VISIT TO

GHUZNI, KABUL
AND
AFGHANISTAN

AND OF A RESIDENCE AT THE
COURT OF

DOST MOHAMED

WITH NOTICES OF RUNJIT SING,
KHIVA AND THE RUSSIAN EXPEDITION

G. T. VIGNE

WITH ILLUSTRATIONS
FROM DRAWINGS MADE BY THE AUTHOR ON THE SPOT

GYAN

Published by

Gyan Publishing House
5, Ansari Road
Daryaganj, New Delhi-110002
Phone: 011-47034999, 9811692060
E-mail: books@gyanbooks.com

Distribution Network
gyanbooks.com
India, USA, Canada, UK, Australia, France

ISBN : 978-81-212-3885-4 (PB)
First Published, London, 1840

2nd Impression 2020

Printed at: Gyan Press, Delhi.

A Personal Narrative of a Visit to Ghuzni, Kabul
and
Afghanistan and of A Residence at the Court of
Dost Mohamed
with Notices of Runjit Sing, Khiva and the Russian Expedition
Author: G. T. Vigne

A PERSONAL NARRATIVE

OF A VISIT TO

GHUZNI, KABUL, AND AFGHANISTAN,

AND OF A

RESIDENCE AT THE COURT OF DOST MOHAMED:

WITH

NOTICES OF RUNJIT SING, KHIVA, AND

THE RUSSIAN EXPEDITION

BY

G. T. VIGNE, Esq. F.G.S.

WITH ILLUSTRATIONS,

FROM DRAWINGS MADE BY THE AUTHOR ON THE SPOT.

Tritum viatorum compitum calca; et, cum poteris, desére.

GRAY'S LETTERS.

LONDON: WHITTAKER & Co. AVE MARIA LANE.

1840.

TO

WILLIAM ASTELL, Esquire,

OF EVERTON HOUSE, BEDFORDSHIRE,

FORTY YEARS AN ACTIVE DIRECTOR OF THE AFFAIRS

OF THE HON. EAST INDIA COMPANY,

IS INSCRIBED,

RESPECTFULLY AND AFFECTIONATELY,

THIS PERSONAL NARRATIVE OF TRAVELS

INTO COUNTRIES LONG SINCE

MORE OR LESS CONNECTED WITH THOSE WHICH ARE

SUBJECT TO BRITISH DOMINION IN ASIA,

AND NOW MADE PRE-EMINENTLY INTERESTING

BY RECENT EVENTS, AND

THE SUCCESSES OF HER MAJESTY'S ARMY.

PREFACE.

The important events which have lately taken place in Afghanistan determined me to publish my Travels in that country, in a first and separate volume; and to reserve, for a subsequent work, those parts of my manuscript which relate to Kashmir, Great and Little Tibet, the mountain-banks of the Indus, and Alpine India north of the Punjab.

I have made my remarks without the smallest regard to party considerations.

To Horace Hayman Wilson, Esq., Professor of Sanscrit in the University of Oxford, I am greatly indebted, for much liberal and valuable assistance; and I also feel myself much obliged to Mr. Masson, the numismatologist, for information he gave me at Kabul regarding the people and the country, which his long residence there, as the Correspondent of the Honourable East-India Company, enabled him to acquire, and which no one was, I believe, more competent to afford than himself.

I took various bearings in my passage through the Sulimani range, but the intense heat prevented me from making a regular map of the route; and I have, therefore, in order to render the small one inserted in this work as complete as possible, made use of that published by Dr. Martin Honninberger, in the Calcutta Asiatic Society's Journal, for April, 1834, and avail myself of this opportunity to thank him for the assistance I have derived from it.

I have only to add, that I have generally followed the latest and most approved method of spelling Asiatic names and words, by the substitution of Italian for English double vowels.

CONTENTS.

CHAPTER I.

CHAPTER II.

CHAPTER III.

CHAPTER IV.

CHAPTER V.

CHAPTER VI.

CHAPTER VII.

CHAPTER VIII.

CHAPTER IX.

CHAPTER X.

CHAPTER XI.

CHAPTER XII.

ILLUSTRATIONS.

ERRATUM.

For "Border Tower," on Vignette, p. 35, *read* "Buddhist Topes at Seiab."

For "Mahomed Khan," *read* "Mohamed Khan."

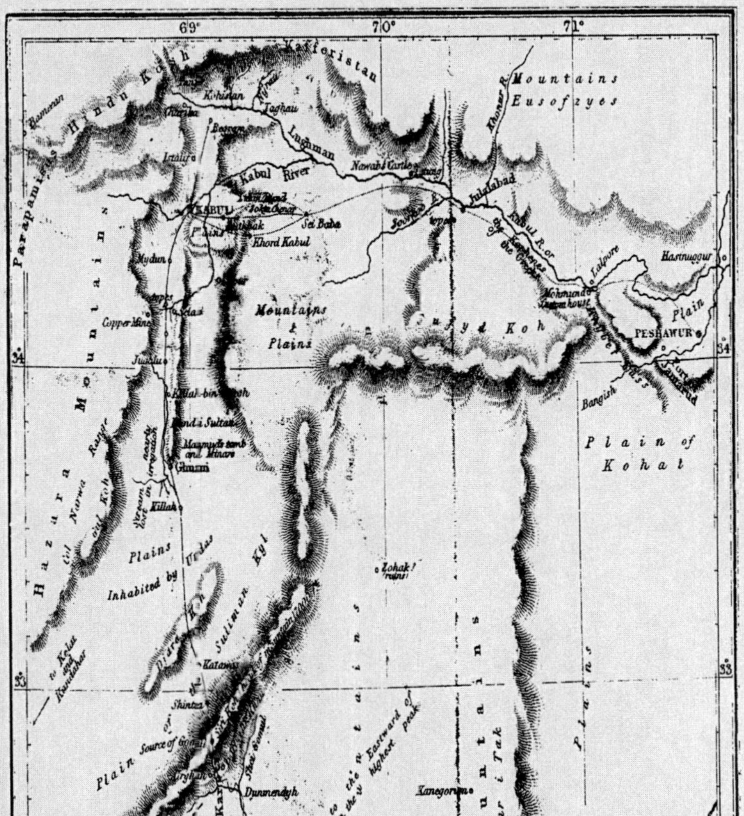

Published by Whittaker & Co. Ave Maria Lane March 1840.

J. & C. Walker Sculp.

THE TOMB OF SULTAN MAHMUD.

CHAPTER I.

Prepare to depart for Multan—Guja Sing—Fête Champêtre—The Lodiana School—Shah Shuja and Shah Ziman—Cross the Sutlij—Altars of Alexander—Description of the Punjab Country—Gardens of Multan—Shrine of the Faquir Shums-i-Tabriz—Heat of Climate—Description of Multan—Mussulman Tombs—Manufactures of Multan—Saman Mul—The Besak—Ameer Khan—The River Teenmu—Proceed to Karur—Huts of the Villages—Cross the Sinde—Ferries over the Indus—Arrival at Purawur—Tufan.

After returning to Lodiana from my first visit to Kashmir and Little Tibet, in eighteen hundred and thirty-five, I formed a design of visiting Kabul. The direct route would have been through Lahore and Peshawur; but my principal reason for not taking that road was, that I had been wandering in Kashmir, Little Tibet, and the Maharajah Runjit Sing's territories, for the best part of the year. I had been considered and treated as his guest, and had taken leave of him in his capital but a month or two before.

On the twelfth of March, 1836, I quitted the hospitable roof of my friend, Captain (now Sir Claude Martine) Wade, and left Lodiana for Multan, intending to proceed thence through the Sulimani mountains to Kabul, in company with the Lohani kafilas, or caravans, after having delayed my departure for a few days, in order to be present at the return of the mission which Runjit Sing had sent to Calcutta, with presents for the King and Governor-General. Lallah Govind Jus, a confidential servant of the Maharajah, was its chief. Guja Sing, the second in importance, was a well-looking and intelligent young dandy, often wearing the splendid yellow dress of the Sikhs, and sometimes the full uniform of a British general officer. He had a great turn for mechanics, and exhibited a theodolite of his own making; and a model of the steam-engine, made for him by Mr. Prinsep, of Calcutta. He affected to say, at least so I was informed, that he had seen little that was new there, excepting the ships of war, which he allowed were wonderful; but it was too evident that he well-knew he had only to recross the Sutlij to astonish his inquiring countrymen, and when discoursing on his favourite topic, mechanics, the energy of his manner, and his animated conversation were certainly not the offspring of oriental indifference. About two years ago, at Amritsir, he fell from a window into the street when intoxicated, and was killed. It would seem that he was desperately bent upon procuring an English wife. He fell in love with a lady at Calcutta; and was, it is said, prevented from marrying her only because it became known that he had already two or three wives in the Punjab. He wished to have remained there altogether, but Runjit sent down a request that nothing of the kind should be allowed; and even went so far as to desire that he should be put under arrest, if he persisted in the latter determination. On his return, he commenced, without knowing one syllable of English, a serious flirtation in the language of the eyes (which seems to be the same all over the world) with some lady at Delhi.

Before I started, I was present at a fête champêtre given by Captain Wade, upon the occasion of the arrival of the mission. There was native dancing, singing, and sword playing. All the beauty and fashion of Lodiana were assembled to see the fireworks and illuminations. Characters from all quarters beyond the Sutlij were also present, magnificent Sikhs, scheming Kashmirians, pensioned Afghans, and supplicant envoys from Great and Little Tibet. The next morning there was an examination of the boys of the Lodiana school, conducted by the Rev. Messrs. Wilson and Newton, the American missionaries, who deserve the greatest credit, and something more, for their voluntary superintendence, and its results. To say nothing of the surprising answers given by the students, particularly to geographical questions, the examination was well worth attending, if it were merely to see the motley assemblage of which the school was composed. The first in rank was the young Nawab Abdul Ghias Khan, nephew of Dost Mahomed Khan of Kabul. Next to him came three or four young Sikhs of an ennobled family—amongst them was Bissen Sing, a nephew of Kosheal Sing, Runjit Sing's chief jemadar, or captain, as he is called, *par-excellence;* and also a son of Kissenchund, the Sikh Vakeel or envoy resident at Lodiana. The rest of the school was composed of rising young Munshis and Baboos of great promise. After reading a passage in English, the boys were required to translate it carefully into Hindustani, and this was usually done with great correctness, and very little hesitation. Upon my return to Lodiana this year, I found that the school existed no more. The parents of the boys, Mussulmen and Hindus, had become alarmed at the enforced observance of Christian religious exercises, and withdrew their children from the school altogether.

Baron Hugel, with whom I had travelled from Kashmir, and myself, were introduced by Captain Wade to Shah Shuja and Shah Ziman, the pensioned ex-kings of the country I was going to visit. We found Shah Shuja sitting on a chair, in a recess, or rather doorway, of his house, with a vista, formed by two rows of attendants, that diverged from it as from a centre. He appeared to be a man aged about fifty, of the middle size, good-natured, and port-wine complexioned, looking more like a gentleman who had lost an estate, than a monarch who had lost his kingdom. He wore a dark-coloured robe, a white turban, and white cotton gloves. Baron Hugel had been received with great distinction by Runjit Sing; I had come in for a share of it; every application which the Shah made to the

Government went through Captain Wade; and yet he allowed neither of us a chair, but kept us standing the whole time. His brother, Shah Ziman, resided in a different part of the building: we went to see him also: we stood; he sat on the ground, pale, thin, dejected, and counting his beads. He asked much about Kashmir, and said that the shawls were not now so fine as they used to be. "I remember," he said, "when the finer fabric could be drawn through a ring." He was praising the beauty of Kashmir. "Yes," remarked the poor blind monarch, "Kashmir is certainly beautiful, and the air and water are good; but," he continued, with a melancholy shake of the head, and a sigh as deep as I ever heard, "Kabul, Kabul! what is Kashmir to Kabul! and I shall never see it again!" We were surprised to hear from Captain Wade, that in spite of their common misfortunes and fate, the two brothers were not on the best terms with each other. The next morning, Shah Shuja sent us several trays, containing the best display of native cookery that I had seen in the East; it had probably been superintended in management by the ladies of the haram.

I think Lodiana the most interesting station in India, and that Captain Wade held the most important appointment, as political agent to the Sikhs.

After a night's dâk, or journey in a palanquin, I found myself at the village of Dhurmkote, and my horse in waiting for me. Two days' ride, over a flat and fertile country, brought me to Firozpore, a place only remarkable for the lofty walls of its fort; which, in the distance, appeared to rise from the plain like a thick and regular clump of trees. Since the late meeting of Lord Auckland and Runjit Sing, it has been put in a state of repair, and a new cantonment has been formed there, as being the nearest place to the Sikh capital, Lahore; thither, too, in case of need, the British cavalry and horse-artillery could arrive in a few hours after crossing the river.

The next day, I was ferried across the Sutlij, after an hour's ride from the town. The river here is somewhat more than two hundred yards in width, from the Punjab side; and it was then so shallow, that the ferrymen jumped into the water, to assist in dragging the boat ashore. The banks all around were flat, sandy, and uninteresting. On the same day, I arrived at Gullah, about seven miles in the interior; and from thence passed through Pak Patan, a considerable village, built on a mound, rising alone from a perfect flat. The last place mentioned by Arrian and Quintus Curtius, in their account of Alexander's march towards the Sutlij, is Sangala. Mr. Masson, who had visited the ruins of Hurripore, or "the green city," a few hours' march from the eastern bank of the Ravee, assured me that he felt quite convinced of this having been the site of Sangala; and that a hill, and a lake, and other localities mentioned in the description of Alexander's victory over the Kathai, were then existing, in such a relative position to each other as to correspond exactly with the account given of Sangala by those authors. It may be inferred, from what follows, that Alexander went thence directly towards the Sutlij, and built his celebrated altars. Pak Patan lies exactly east of Hurripore. But Alexander was surely too anxious about his glory to have built his altars on the plains of India, where they would be washed away by the river, which is constantly changing its course, otherwise I should have been very much inclined, with all deference, to have placed them at Pak Patan: the name signifies, literally, "the clean ferry;" whence we should imagine that the river once flowed close to it. It is now a few miles from the Sutlij, and the country is covered with a low jungle; but the lofty mound on which the village has gradually risen cannot but suggest the idea of a substratum of ruins; and the place derived an interest in my eyes upon the mere possibility of what those ruins might be. I think it probable that Alexander would rather have followed up the course of the Sutlij, for the purpose of building his altars upon the solid rock of the Himalaya. I believe that the trench and ruins first visited by Mr. Moorcroft upon the Sekunder,—the Dhar, or hill of Alexander, near the Mundeh country,—are the remains of his celebrated altars. Place and probability are well in accordance with this opinion; but I shall reserve a more lengthened dissertation on the subject, and on the position of the rock of Aomos, until I treat of my journeys to Kashmir and Tibet.

My next stations were Tibi, Lukhoki, Luka, Suldera, Tiba, and Mukdam-Ram. Six miles beyond the latter place the domes of Multan were visible over the jungle. I arrived there on the sixth of April, after a very uninteresting march, though without accident or robbery. Thanks to Captain Wade and Kissen Chund, Runjit Sing's vakeel at Lodiana, I had been furnished with a sufficient guard. There was a perfect flat or plain throughout the whole distance, much was in cultivation, but more was jungle, composed principally of a prickly mimosa, tamarisk, and byr-apple or jujube growing in isolated bushes, on a hard and sun-glazed soil. Where there was cultivation, the Persian wells were seen and heard constantly at work, for the purposes of irrigation. The crops, chiefly of wheat and barley, were every where green, and looking remarkably well; those in the Punjab were, I think, the finest; the wheat in particular, which grew here, had no stunted stalk, and was often as high and as fine-looking as I have ever seen it in Europe; but the Lahore wheat has always been celebrated. In the jungle were antelopes, hares, and black and grey partridges (francolins), in great abundance. Tigers are to be found in some parts of the jungle, and on the banks of the river. I did not hear of any lions, but I have known small ones to be bayonetted by Runjit Sing's hunting Sepahis, within two days' march of Lahore, and have seen their skins.

Upon my arrival at Multan, I was domiciled in a Bara-Deri (twelve doors) or summer house in the Bagh-i-Begi, made by the Nawab Surfuras Khan, about thirty years ago; it was cool, well-shaded with orange trees, and laid out in the usual manner, with reservoirs and fountains. The walks, intersecting each other at right angles, were raised above the parterres and flower-beds, that they might be dry when the latter are covered with water. There are numerous gardens in the environs of Multan, often formed around the shrine of some Mussulman Faquir; and no man will quarrel with the fanaticism which has procured him shade and shelter in the climate of India. In the Hazur-i-Bagh, or the garden of the Presence, on the north side of the Fort, I saw a large tree, the Mowul-Siri, grown, as they told me, from a cutting, which was originally brought from Mecca; but I do not vouch for the truth of the story. The principal shrine is that of the Faquir Shums-i-Tabriz; Shums signifies the sun in Persia. This holy man, they say, poor and wretched, made his appearance in the bazaar at Multan, and going to a Tabaki or cook's shop, requested permission to dress his dinner, which was rudely denied him. A similar request was made to another, and was met by a similar rebuff. The Faquir, proud and indignant, called upon the sun to descend from heaven. The obedient luminary appeared in the air above the bazaar, and he cooked his dinner in its rays. The scorched and exhausted inhabitants of Multan crawled to him in terror, and implored him to send the sun on high again; a request with which he at length thought proper to comply. Sir J. Malcolm, in his History of Persia, affirms that Shums-i-Tabriz was a great man of the sect of the Sufis, or oriental philosophers or free-thinkers. They believe in one God, and the doctrine of predestination, and generally deny the existence of future rewards and punishments;

believing the soul after death to be re-absorbed into the Divine essence. Some of this sect affirm that Christ was a Sufi.

After this, it is not surprising that Multan should be found notoriously hot; it is further a very dry place, although nearly within the full influence of the tropical rains of India: and it was singular that scarcely any had fallen for two years lately. I was, however, fortunate in the weather, which was cooled by repeated showers, so that the thermometer averaged only seventy-six degrees in the shade for the ten days, between the sixth and sixteenth of April, that I was there.

Multan, supposed to be the capital of the Malli, of Alexander's historians, is a dusty and slovenly-looking city, containing about forty-five thousand inhabitants. The streets are narrow, and the houses are two, three, and four stories high; flat-roofed of course, and built of sun-burnt brick, with a washing of mud over them. The city wall, about five-and-thirty feet high, is of the same material, but in a decayed state. Around Multan, in various directions, are numerous hollow ways of no depth, connected by a short cut or hole through the bank, when necessary. In the hot weather these are filled by means of a deep canal which communicates with the river Chenab. The Fort was built by Buran Bey, the son of the Emperor Jehan Guire, upon a mound that rises in the north part of the city, of which it occupies a considerable portion; the city is about three miles in circumference.

There are four gates, one of which is closed up by the order of the Maharajah Runjit Sing. The walls of the Fort, which in some places are sixty feet in height, with bastions at intervals of about seventy yards, are in good repair, but mounted with a total of only six or seven ill-cast native guns. They have been surrounded by a ditch, in many places entirely destroyed. In the interior of the Fort is the shrine of Mir Singh Puree, a Hindoo saint, and two lofty and spacious buildings erected over the tombs of two Mussulmen saints of great celebrity — Bhawul-Huk and Shah Allum. The ground-plan of one is an octagon, with a diagonal of about eighteen yards, and buttresses at the angles. The lower part of the building is surmounted with another octagon and a dome rising to the height of a hundred feet. The whole of the outside is tastefully ornamented with coloured tiles, chiefly blue,.in imitation of those of China. They were originally used in ornamenting the public buildings of Multan, and were made there; but there is now no other manufactory of them nearer than Delhi. Runjit Sing's cannon appear to have told with great effect upon the roofs of the principal mosques. Most of the buildings of the Fort were destroyed after the capture of the city, with the exception of these shrines and the house of Mazuffer Khan, which stands on the most elevated part of it, and commands an extensive view. This brave man, the last independent Nawab of Multan, lies buried in the Vestibule of Bhawul-Huk. For twelve years he resolutely opposed the inroads of the Sikhs, but the Fort was at last taken in the year one thousand eight hundred and eighteen, by Kurruk Sing, the only son of Runjit, and present ruler of the Punjab. Mazuffer Khan fought in person at the Kederi gate of the Fort, and at last fell mortally wounded, after a desperate resistance. When Runjit Sing visited his tomb afterwards, he is reported to have made a speech somewhat of the same nature with that uttered by Napoleon at the tomb of Frederick of Prussia.

Multan is famous for its silk manufactures. I visited the house of a weaver; it presented a very different appearance from the atelier of a shawl-maker in Kashmir: there I have seen twenty men at work in one room, here there are seldom more than three, who sit in a hollow in the ground, by which means their hands are brought down even with the tanee or woof, which is extended near the floor and fastened to a post not more than a foot in height. This apparatus takes up a great deal of room, whereas the frame of the shawl-worker, which is perpendicular, does not occupy a space of more than six square yards. Seven hundred maunds of raw silk are brought to Multan every year by the Lohanis, chiefly from Bokhara and Turkistan: these are manufactured in one hundred and fifty workshops. One man will finish an ordinary kaish or piece of silk in six days, perhaps three yards long and a foot and a half wide, taking eight days previously for the arrangement of the weaving apparatus. A very handsome kaish is finished in sixteen days. That of the red colour is most valuable, it is dyed with cochineal, which is brought from either Bombay or Bokhara; that from Bombay is one rupee a seer—about a shilling a pound. Multan is also famous for its carpets and embroidery.

There are from a thousand to fifteen hundred maunds of tobacco produced around Multan annually. The best, which is called suruk, or the red, is sold for six annas, equal to about nine pence. Inferior kinds are sold from four to two annas a seer.

I exchanged visits with Saman Mul, the governor of Multan: Runjit Sing has been heard to say, that he was one of the best officers in his service. Whilst I was at Multan, he sent me a kilaat or dress of honour, together with an elephant, and a couple of horses for my use, as an especial mark of his favour. He is a thin man, with a good tempered, and, for a native, a superior expression of countenance, and is said to have distinguished himself at the taking of the city. His government was well-spoken of by the Lohani merchants, who gave him an excellent character for justice in his dealings with them. He is the arch opponent of the minister Rajah Dhihan Sing, and his brothers Gulab and Sucheyt Sing, whose influence at the court of Runjit is usually all-powerful.

On the eleventh of April, the Besak, a Hindoo festival, took place in the morning;

I rode to the river, about three miles distant. The country which intervenes between the city and its banks was looking very green and picturesque, considering it is entirely flat: a great deal of land was under cultivation and bearing very fine crops of wheat. Well-planted gardens were always in sight; and date and palm-trees standing singly or in groups, were frequently seen amongst the numerous topes or clumps of mulberry, mango, banian, peepul, and acacia trees. By the roadside were the venders of wreaths and fans made from the flags that grew on the water's edge. In the afternoon there was a fair in the Bagh Ali Akber, a garden with a shrine of a Fakir of that name. I saw the Multanis returning; every species of conveyance had, of course, been put in requisition, horses, mules, donkeys, carrying one or two persons, camels, each bearing seven or eight women and children, disposed on either side in trucks, and unlicensed bullock carts, with cargoes of giggling dancing girls. The number of persons who will stow themselves in these vehicles is quite astounding; all were in their holiday dresses. The Hindoo was to be distinguished by his cast-mark on his forehead, his rose-coloured turban, and red flowing trousers. The Multan Mussulman usually wore a white dress, of the same kind of pattern. The Sikh, generally a Sepahi, was recognised by his sword, matchlock, and accoutrements; his scanty turban, his earrings, his would-be knee breeches, or his close fitting ill-made trousers. The Lohanis, my future fellow-travellers, were conspicuous, by reason of the snake-like folds of their turban, and by their dark, swarthy, and manly features beneath them. Ferishta says, that Multan was three or four times chastised by Mahmoud of Ghuzni, for revolt, and that he marched thence across the Desert, in his way to Guzerat and Somnath.

I quitted Multan the seventeenth of April, in company with Ameer Khan, a Lohani of the highest rank, who had one of the noblest countenances I ever beheld. I was introduced to him at Lodiana, by Captain Wade. We were ferried over the river at the Rajghat in a large and clumsy, but useful boat. The Teenmu (three months), for so the stream is called, is formed by an union of the Chenab, the Jalum, and the Ravee, the two first forming a junction with each other about forty miles above Ahmedpore, receiving the Ravee at that place, which is, I believe, also about the same distance from Multan. The Teenmu is hardly a third part of the stream of the Indus, and yet at Multan it is half a mile in width: though much indebted to its sands and islands for this expanse, it is certainly a very large body of water, the main stream running beneath the right bank, with a depth of about five or six yards. After a fine morning's march, over a flat and desert country, with little shade, and very bad water, I arrived at Larga, a small, but neat-looking town, built of mud and brick, and nearly equi-distant from Dhera Ghazi Khan, and Dhera Ismael Khan. For twenty miles previously, I had a distant view of the Sulimani mountains, on the opposite side of the Indus, running, apparently, from the north-west to the south-east. The weather was hazy, and I could distinguish little besides a low waved out-line. At Larga, I saw the sun set directly behind the Kayser or Tukt-i-Suliman mountain, distant about sixty miles. I here learned that the Maharajah had marched ten thousand men, under the command of Rajah Sucheyt Sing, into the mountain district of Bunu, lying to the north of Karabagh. My next stage was Karur. At a village called Radal, I accidentally noticed a Zwanjera tree, producing a red gum, called, I think Chyr; it was common, I was told, at Multan, but not in India. Karur resembles Larga, but is smaller: it stands on the edge of a plain, covered with the tufts of the gigantic grass, of which the huts throughout this country are made. They look like huge half barrels of straw, hooped with cables of the same material. The district is not destitute of villages. In the jungle, I nearly run foul of a Cobra, whose motionless head was raised above the bush, in which his body was concealed, and bore so much resemblance to a dead branch, that I did not perceive what it was, until I was close upon him.

On both sides of the river we passed a

tamarisk jungle, swarming with wild boars. The ground was hard and dry at this season, but in June, when the river is swollen by the rains, that fall in the mountains, it causes such a flood that a boat can be piloted from Kurur for fifteen miles, to a village on the opposite side, and parallel with the banks for a much greater distance. I was first ferried over a small branch of the Sinde, about a hundred yards in width and seven feet in depth. We then rode for nearly a mile over an island of sand, and arrived at the Kyaree or Putah Ghat, where there is a ferry over the main stream. A grass hut, erected by the ferryman, afforded a shelter from the heat. The thermometer stood at one hundred degrees in the sun, by the boiling scale; and I should estimate the elevation at about eight hundred feet. The Sinde, Indus, or Attok, is here about three quarters of a mile in width, deep, and not very muddy, containing, I should think, at least half as much water again as any other stream of the Punjaba, running at the rate of nearly three miles an hour. The name Attok is derived from Atkana, or Atukna, signifying in Hindustani, *to stop*; no pious Hindoo will venture to go beyond it of his own accord, for fear of losing caste. From the mountains downward to the junction at Mittunkote, it is called the Sinde, or Abu Sin, "the father river." There is upon record an account of a Hindu or Sikh force, that chased a party of Mussulmen across the Indus, but refused to follow up their success by crossing it themselves. I regret that I did not make a note of the circumstance when it was related to me, but it may be known to many of my oriental readers. Such is the wonderful attachment to the British uniform, which they are proud of wearing, that in the late expedition to Afghanistan, the native Sepahis, many of

On Stone by J. B Pyne from a Drawing by the Author

VIEW OF ATTOK FROM THE WESTERN BANK OF THE INDUS.

London. Published by Whittaker & Co Ave Maria Lane.

them Rajpoots, cheered loudly when they saw the British flag flying at Bukkur, and passed the bridge over the Indus with enthusiasm.

Replete with interest from the mountains of Upper Tibet and Karakorun, to its junction with the ocean at Karachi, this vast stream appears to roll over, rather than through, the naked sand of the plains, and where, without it, there would be neither barrier nor boundary; it wanders from the northern to the southern horizon, as if unconscious of its own importance as a line of demarcation, or as a Rubicon alike to the native and the invader of Hindostan.

The Tukt-i-Suliman, or Kayser mountain, bore north-north-west of the ferry, distant about forty miles. There are four large ghats or ferries between the Putla

Ghat, and seven to the south, between it and Dhera Ghazi Khan. The river varies in width, near Karabagh; and it narrows between the hills to about one hundred and sixty yards, with a tranquil stream. Half-a-dozen strong, large, and useful boats, built of the Deodar or hill-cedar, fastened with iron clamps, and ornamented with carving, ply at this ferry, which is the richest of all. I was told that the ferryman received about two thousand five hundred rupees for passage money annually. The Lohanis from Calcutta, Delhi, Jypoor, all take this route to their rendezvous at Derabund. A duty of five per cent. was first levied upon their merchandise at Multan, the same that was paid in the time of Mazuffer Khan; another tax of one rupee, six annas, a maund, is levied at Larga, on behalf of the Maharajah Runjit Sing, and another of six annas was then paid to Mahomed Khan, the Nawab of Dhera Ismael Khan.

After crossing the main stream of the Attok, I found myself on another island, covered with the dwarf tamarisk. I forded the thin shallow stream on the other side of it, and arrived at Purawur. I observed the boys of the village playing a regular English game of peg-top, the pegs were of wood. The Tukt-i-Suliman mountains bore north-west of Purawur.

A furious tufan passed over me at this place, and rendered the air deliciously cool for a day or two afterwards. These sudden storms are common throughout India in the spring. For an hour before sunset, clouds are gathered in the western horizon, which is illuminated with repeated flashes of lightning, accompanied with a continued muttering of distant thunder, the atmosphere becoming oppressively sultry. Suddenly the heavens are furiously agitated, a brightening space is seen on the horizon, and the clouds appear, rapidly diverging from it as from a centre. A few large drops of rain are dashed downwards with great violence, the whirlwind rises almost instantly, and blows as if it blew its last, with a violence to which Europe is a stranger. The rain then falls as if a deluge were commencing: sudden and terrific crashes of thunder are heard above and around, and hail stones, such as we have read of, are often precipitated with most injurious effect. The violence of the tufan is generally exhausted in about half an hour.

BORDER TOWER.

CHAPTER II.

The Kayser Mountain—Village of Gundee and Mound—Ruins—Reach the Lohani camp—Lohani Salutations—High Range of Temperature—Mulberry Bird—Description of the Camp Amusements—Ameer Khan's Stories—Story from the Ferishta—Mahmud Khan's Empire—Runjit Sing's Conquests—The Lohanis—Duties levied on the Merchants—Village of Derabund—Earthquake—The Mountaineers—Mineral Fluid and Mumiar—Mountaineer Attacks.

I NEVER saw a finer morning than that which broke after the storm had passed away. The jungle had disappeared, and I emerged on an open space of vast extent, destitute even of a blade of grass, and as flat as a bowling-green. It seemed to extend, with scarcely any intervening object, to the very foot of the Sulimani range. The Kayser mountain itself was a noble object, far higher and bolder than I expected to find it, and seemed to be a collection of inaccessible precipices. The mountains of Kalabagh, containing the salt mines, were on my right; their isolated tops alone being visible above the horizon. On the north, the Sulimani range was finished by the Pahar, or hills of Koh-i-Tak; and to the north-west was the Koh-i-Kondi, with a little snow upon its summit. The Kayser mountain arose in front, in a southern direction. The Shirami hills appeared to descend into the plain, near Dhera Ghazi Khan. We dismounted at the village of Gundee. Near this place, I saw low mounds or hillocks, rising about thirty feet above the level of the plain, and, in circumference, about a third part of a mile. They are covered with broken bricks and tiles, and are, no doubt, the remains of villages. In the centre of one, I found a large pit, ten yards across, and forty feet deep. I was told, that a few years ago a fakir dreamed that a well was concealed there, which induced Omar Khan, a Lohani chief, to open the pit. He found water, but it was very black; and a well, sunk in the bottom of the pit, was filled by the ground falling in upon it. In the south-eastern corner, an old circular burj, a tower of red brick, exceedingly well-built, arose from the bottom of the pit to the surface, where it was about five feet in diameter. I saw another and a larger mound two miles to the south of Mysozyh, a village which we reached the next day; it lay on the plain, precisely as if it were a mass of clay, that had been dropped from a great height, its sides furrowed by the trickling of rain, and cracked by the action of the sun. The surface was every where covered with bricks, tiles, and Hindu ornaments made of baked clay; so much so, that at first sight it was impossible not to suppose that the place had been a brick kiln, such as is seen near Agra and Delhi. The vicinity of a flat space, similarly covered, served to strengthen such an opinion; but its circumference of half a mile, and its height of fifty feet, were sufficient to assure me that there had been a town on the plain, and that the mound contained the ruins of its protecting fort. Blocks of stone, which had once been squared, and large flat bricks, fifteen inches wide at the larger end, and so shaped as to have belonged to a circular building of seven yards in diameter, were scattered in every direction. I also found numerous fragments of Hindoo idols, particularly of the little humped-back bull. I subsequently set men working to search the remains of another old town, not above a mile from the camp. They brought me nothing but some old pice (halfpence), with the emperor Jehan Guire's name upon them; and some sifted earth, which contained, as they told me, a few minute particles of gold. A fourth, and yet larger dhera, as these mounds are called, exists in the neighbourhood of Derabund; it is perhaps a furlong in length, and rises to about the height of eighty feet above the plain. Close to it are the ruins of a town; and both are washed by a mountain torrent, that has swept away one side of the mound, and formed an overhanging cliff, in which red brick and layers of mortar are to be seen, together with rounded stones taken from the old bed of the torrent, for building purposes. The Thanadar, or chief man of a village, dispatched persons to dig for me, on condition that I should cure his eyes for him, which were not the better for a hot needle that had been drawn between the lids by a Poshtu practitioner. I procured nothing remarkable from this mound. There were five or six more similar to it scattered over the plain. Their formation is not, I think, difficult to account for. Water in these countries is never left to itself: a well is first built; then a village rises; then a fort, usually quadrangular, if we may judge from those of the present day, is created. The well becomes dry and choked up, and the inhabitants leave this home for another, where better water or pasturage has been found; cleared land has proved productive; a new and more advantageous market has been opened, or where the predatory visits of the Vuziri mountaineers have become less frequent. The mud-works of the deserted village crack and crumble in the sun, or are washed away by the rains; the stone-work of the fort, solid and resisting, becomes a nucleus for a bank of sand and dust, which are driven against it with great violence, and in immense quantities, by the tufans, and those whirling pillars of sand seen on a sultry day moving across every plain in Asia. Incipient hillocks, formations of the same kind, may be remarked around the roots of every bush in the country.

On the twenty-seventh of April, we reached the Lohani camp at Mysozyh, a small village protected by two mud forts, into which they could retire in case of an attack by the Nawab of Dhera Ismael Khan. When the kafila or caravan is absent, they perhaps would not find a hundred men to defend the fort, and they would be obliged to retire into the Sulimani mountains for protection. Ameer Khan, my Lohani friend, was soon surrounded by a host of his kinsfolk, men and boys. I was much amused with the formal mode of salutation in use amongst the Lohanis. When they met,—even the oldest friends or relations, it seemed to make no difference,—the oriental embrace was first given; that is, each person passed his head over the left shoulder of the other, and then over the right, so that the breasts were brought in contact. The one then asked the other, in Poshtu I believe, "Shei jur?" "Are you well?" and was answered with the same question; secondly, "Shei pakhair?" "Are you strong?" and was answered again by the same question; thirdly, "Rogu shei?" (I believe), "Are you safe?" and two or three more, were answered in a similar manner; they then embraced again, and the salutation was finished. The women did not appear at first, as, according to the oriental custom, they kept strict purdah; that is, remained veiled and secluded. In the distance they resemble nuns, in their appearance and dress; which consists of a very dark long robe, and a chudur or mantilla of the same colour. Afterwards, on the march, they became less shy, and I was struck with their fine features. Many of them are the offspring of the female slaves, who have been purchased for their beauty in the countries north of the Hindu Kosh. The men were occasionally richly apparelled; they had silks and shawls at command; and though there was often too great a display of finery on their own persons, they did not always exhibit the carriage and bold bearing of the Patan or Afghan soldiers.

All accounts agree that the heat on the plains under the Sulimani range is excessive. The weather, which in the preceding year, at the same season, was so hot that the Lohanis could not remain in their tents, but preferred resting themselves under the scanty shade of the acacias that are scattered over the plain around Mysozyh, was this year much cooler than usual; it was showery and cloudy by turns, with a cool breeze from the north at night. The thermometer, as yet, in my tent, ranged only from eighty-eight degrees to one hundred and three, at noon. I retired for shelter to the gateway of the little fort, which I found was the coolest place, as there the heat never exceeded ninety-two. The Lohanis, who were waiting the arrival of a caravan from Multan, passed their time as they best could. They formed in groups under any shade they could find, chattering, smoking, and sleeping away the hottest part of the day, rarely moving, excepting when aroused by the call to prayers, or to get a chance shot with the pellet bow. A young Lohani is seldom seen without one, and makes good use of it. They are the best shots I ever saw; the bows are made of banswood, sometimes of pustuna, which grows in the Sulimani range; the bans is the bambu ; I do not know what the other is. With these, and round pellets of clay baked in the sun, they will knock over as many as ten small birds in a day. The mulberry bird, or *pastor roseus*, was a frequent victim; and the skin and feathers on the breast were spitted on the bow as trophies. It is a gregarious bird, with the habits of the starling, and of the same size; its plumage is of a dull rose colour, and black. It visits Persia, Afghanistan, and parts of India, in the mulberry season. The young girls amused themselves by swinging; the children splashed and dabbled in the stream. The breeding of horses was not neglected; the donkeys took care of themselves, making a tremendous noise, and chasing each other about, to the great discomfiture of the tents and tent-ropes. The dog, usually a half-bred Bokhara greyhound, ran about open-mouthed from the shade to the water, and then again from the water to the shade. Fresh arrivals from Multan would now and then happen, in the shape of a well-equipped and well-mounted cavalier, or of a string of camels, or a peasant riding upon a cow. On one side of the Attok, the cow is worshipped by the Sikhs, as sacred; on the other, it is useful as a beast of burden, and ridden with a ring in its nose. The sleepers would be disturbed by some beardless catapultist, who, having knocked over a bird with his pellet bow, would scream out lustily for a chaku, or penknife, in order to cut its throat before it was dead, and make it "hulal," that is, lawful eating. Sometimes a horse would break loose from his picketing ropes, neighing joyously, and dashing with speed through the camp; or an angry camel, whose leg had been tied up, would snap the rope that confined him, and scamper at a long trot over the plain, attended by two or three horsemen, who, having mounted in hot haste, were trying to turn him with their spears, and also by forty or fifty men on foot, two or three of whom would hang on by the tail at the same time, until he was secured. In the evening, the camels, sheep, and goats, that had been out browsing the whole day, were driven into the camp for security. When the mania for staring at me—the Feringi—was over, I was comfortable enough, lying in the coolest place I could find, with my books, drawing and writing materials around me, unmolested, excepting when asked for medicines. I was glad to hear that common medicine, such as senna, could be purchased in every bazaar; and that leeches were generally procurable, far or near. I often administered sulphur, but calomel only in extreme cases.

Ameer Khan was the only person who would sit in a chair before me; and in the cool of the evening, I usually sent for him, to listen to his stories about Kabul, and the countries north of the Hindu Kosh. How the king of Bokhara, Bahadur Khan, in his conduct and decisions, acted up to the letter of the Koran. How he was attended, as he rode through the streets; and how the people gave him their most respectful salaam. How a man who drank there, was punished by so many stripes, (I forget how many), for the first offence, so many for the second, and by death for the third; and how tobacco and wine were used in secret. How at the festival of the Ede, the king, like Solomon of old, at the consecration of the temple, stood in front of the people, who were ranged by thousands, on the plain of the Edegar; and how, when he gave the signal, the inferior Mullahs listened to his words, and watched the time of prostration, praying when he prayed, and kneeling when he knelt. How the earth was supported on a cow, and the cow stood upon the water; and how hot and cold were breathed forth by two enormous serpents. How Alexander the Great was a Mussulman, and that the Mullah was ready to tell me so! That the reason, why the Hindus take such pains in cleaning their teeth, is, that they are trying to purify themselves from the taint which their ancestors acquired, when Mahmud, of Ghuzni, played them a trick, and made them unconsciously eat the dust of the pounded idol, at Somnath; and how the same great man, in the plenitude of his pride and power, commanded a fakir, who was renowned for his learning, to tell him without fail by to-morrow's dawn, and under the threat of a heavy punishment, where the centre of the world was! and how the terrified and puzzled fakir was relieved by the advice which his daughter gave him; and how, in accordance with it, on the next morning, the fakir boldly advanced, in full durbar to the throne of Mahmud, and striking his staff into the ground, at the monarch's feet, exclaimed there was the "centre of the world!" And how his address and wisdom were rewarded by the flattered Mahmud, and how he was applauded by the courtiers, who dared not dispute the point with him, by saying that the centre of the universe was not at Mahmud's feet. Ferishta says, that the king had one night, in a debauch, cut off the long tresses of his favourite mistress, and was much concerned the next morning for what he had done: he sat, rose, and walked by turns, and his attendants were too much alarmed to approach him. The philosopher and poet Unsuri, accosted him with some extempore lines, which so pleased the king, that he ordered his mouth to be three times filled with jewels; and then calling for wine, he sat with the poet and washed down his grief.

Mahmud Khan, the powerful chief of Dhera Ismael Khan and Mazuffer Khan, the brave defender of Multan, were brothers of the family of the Sirdoyze. Mahmud Khan's territories extended from Mohamed Wallah, ten miles on the west of Multan, to Dhera Bund, at the foot of the Sulimani range, and from Mohmund Kote on the south, to the hills of Karabagh, fifty miles above Dhera Ismael Khan. Four years after the death of Mahmud Khan, who could bring several thousand cavalry into the field, Runjit Sing took the country, after a faint resistance of twenty days, having first invested and captured Munkera, a strong fort on the Punjab side of the Attok. The present Nawab Shere Mahomed Khan is a grandson of Mahmud Khan, and then held the country, on payment to the Maharajah, of forty, fifty, or a hundred thousand rupees yearly. How completely has the discipline of the Sikhs, and the talents of their extraordinary ruler, overthrown the power of the Afghans on the line of the Indus. Multan, Shikapore, Dhera Ghazi Khan, were taken when Jabar Khan, the brother of Dost Mahomed Khan, of Kabul, was governor, to say nothing of the conquest of Kashmir and Peshawur; and although Runjit had not occupied Sinde, yet his successes had emboldened the Ameers to refuse their tribute to Kabul; they have paid none since Shah Shuja-ul-Mulkh, when in possession of the throne of Kabul, visited Sinde and Kandahar, for the purpose of collecting money to defray the expenses of the war in which he lost his crown. After the taking of Mankera, Khuruk Sing crossed the Attok at the Kyari Ghat, on a predatory expedition, and carried away more than a lak of rupees. Five years afterwards, the country was successively visited by Kosheal Sing, Tarah Chund, and No Nehal Sing, the present heir-apparent of the Punjab.

The Lohanis are descended from Lohani or Luhur, the son of Miani, a Mussulman shepherd, or goat-herd of Ghor, or Mushkon, a district east of Herat, who lived in the time of Mahmud, of Ghuzni. Lohani had two wives; Syri, by whom he had Morwut; and Turi, by whom he had five sons; Muma, Meya, Tatur, Panuch, and Hud, who had no children. Muma had three sons; Yakub, Yasin, and Hyder. The descendants of Yakub are called the Yakul Kyl. Yasin had two sons; Dowlut and Hassan. Hyder had four sons; whence the Zukukyl, Pura Kyl, Ibrahim Kyl, and Kurzi. The Lohanis consider one or other of the names just mentioned, as the founder of their family. These Lohanis, who are descended from Meya, called themselves the Meya Kyl. The next are the Tatur Kyl, and the Panuch Kyl. Lohani himself was a wandering trader. There were Lohanis, the sons of Miani, with Mahmud of Ghuzni, who returned with him after his victories in Hindustan; Mahmud's son was Sultan Mahomed. Sultan Masud, who succeeded, had no sons; and about this time, the Lohanis were placed at Derabund, which was given to them. From that time to this, they have traded between Hindustan and Kabul; and they are real men of business. Such is their own account.

When the danger of the march through the mountains is over, they think of nothing but the price of goods. I never showed them anything, whether intended as a present or not, but the first question was, what may be the price of that in London or Calcutta? At Kabul, they will come to the house of a debtor with a pair of scales, perhaps a month or two before the payment is due; and, by making up a good story, will sometimes screw out the money beforehand. If they sell a poor Afghan an ox, for instance, at a year's credit, the creditor, with two or three of his friends, will take care to wait upon their debtor in due time, treating him with great courtesy, and perhaps observing some delicacy in making their demands; but they compel payment of the money, by residing in the poor man's house, as his guests, till the cash be forthcoming, as the laws of hospitality will not permit him to turn them out.

Runjit Sing has since taken the country belonging to the Nawab of Dhera Ismael Khan, but the Lohanis were constantly in hot water with the Nawab; and on the eve of departure, we were nearly delayed by his detention of some camels, until a certain sum was paid for them. Some years since, they determined to resist his exorbitant taxation of their merchandise. I was informed that he entered their country around, with three thousand men, and seven pieces of cannon. The Lohanis assembled from all quarters, and were more than numerically equal to the invader. They fired at each other for twenty-four hours; but the Lohanis had the advantage, as the lights which he burnt enabled them to pick off his men during the night. The Lohanis—such is their own account—lost two hundred and fifty men; and the Nawab was obliged to retreat, with the loss of four hundred, two or three of his cannon, and with a diminished revenue. Thenceforth the duties paid by the Sirdagurs, or Lohani merchants, were reduced from nine to six annas a maund for their cloth goods, from eight to six rupees for every sale camel, and from five to three for every sale horse: and the impost levied at Derabund was reduced from one thousand four hundred, to one thousand one hundred, rupees a-year. The monarchs of Kabul were more lenient, exacting only five thousand rupees yearly, for the two villages of Derabund and Mysozyh. I do not quite vouch for the accuracy of these statements, having heard of them only from the Lohanis themselves.

Derabund is a wretched looking village, a collection of low mud walls, well watered by a mountain stream, and tolerably sheltered by a few mimosa and tamarisk trees. It is surprising that no mango topes, or clumps, have been planted, considering how long the Lohanis have dealt with the country as their own, and the great heat to which they and their families are exposed, and how much beholden they are to shade for their health and comfort. The slope of the plain is the most deceitful I have ever seen. As the Attok pursues its course some distance from the mountains, there can be no doubt that the ground descends from them to the river; but I could hardly believe it to be the case, had I not seen stream after stream running downwards. Derabund and Mysozyh are just sufficiently distant to command what may be termed an horizon between them and the mountains; and the real declivity being very slight, the ground appears to drop a little on the other side of it.

Derabund was much injured by an earthquake which occurred five years back, early in the spring. It was felt from Peshawur to Dhera Ghazi Khan, but the centre of its violence was at Derabund. Camels and horses could not stand; water appeared from crevices that opened in the plain; and fragments of loosened rock fell in several places amongst the mountains. I wished very much to have ascended the Kayser, or Tukt-i-Suliman; but, after all, my attempts at arrangements for that purpose were unsuccessful. They first talked of a very numerous guard, which was to be hired at an expense I did not choose to incur; the company of a mullah, or holy man, was then suggested, but when it came to the point, he said he could not answer for my safety without a sufficient escort. There would be a certainty of detention until a large sum of money was paid, the paths were few and difficult, and there was no possibility of avoiding the mountaineers, who were numerous and lawless. Tyranny is better than anarchy, and any government is better than no government at all,—so says a high legal authority. Had there been a chief, although a robber, he might have been bribed and flattered, by the honour of receiving a Feringi. It might have been in my power to have asked a boon for him at the hands of Dost Mahomed Khan, or the Nawab of Dhera. But the inhabitants of these mountains, throughout their whole extent, own little authority but those of their mullahs, who are supposed to decide with honour, even amongst thieves. The Tukt-i-Suliman, from the plains, appears to be a serrated ridge, mural and perpendicular near the top, shaped somewhat like a horse-shoe, with a circular end to the north. It rises much above any other mountains in sight. The Lohanis say it is higher than any hill between Derabund and Kabul. The loftiest part is to the north-west; and as it sinks a little on the north-east quarter, the double ridge is discernible from the latter place. Derabund being about seven hundred feet above the level of the sea, as far as I can trust the measurement that I ventured to make from the plains, I should

On Stone by J. B Pyne from a Drawing by the Author

VIEW OF THE TUKT-I-SULIMAN MOUNTAIN WITH PART OF THE LOHANI CAMP AT DERABUND.

London. Published by Whittaker & C° Ave Maria Lane.

estimate the height of the ridge to be about nine thousand feet more. Dark and finely pencilled lines were visible for about two-thirds of the height of the ridge. These, when seen through a glass, proved to be rows of fir-trees, waving as they projected or receded, with the ravines and banks on its side; a few only were growing on the sheltering crevices upon the summit, which, in the distance, appeared to be of a bare, light-coloured, grey rock. I was told, that on the top, there was a holy stone or rock, the seat of a Mussulman Fakir, whose name it bears; but I venture to doubt the story.

My inquiries for natural curiosities were not wholly unsuccessful. Ameer Khan sent into the mountains for some mineral liquor, which he told me was collected by dipping cotton into the places where it oozed through the ground. I thought immediately that it was water which had passed through a bed of mumiai, the asphaltum so well known in India, by the natives, under the name of "negro's fat[1]." The natives of India believe that mumiai is procured from a negro's

[1] Mr. Edward Solly, Jun., of the Royal Asiatic Society, has favoured me with the following notice. "The fluid is of a honey-brown colour; at the temperature of 55° Fahr. (when I examined it); it is of about the consistence and degree of transparency of honey. When it is warmed to a little above 60°, it becomes limpid, and nearly transparent; when cooled, it becomes more and more viscid, and finally solid. Rubbed on the skin, it feels greasy, in the manner peculiar to naphtha; it stains paper like an oil. Its specific gravity, at 60° is =0·8491; and it, in consequence, floats upon the surface of water. At the common temperature (*i. e.* below 70°), it gives off very little vapour, and therefore does not inflame on the approach of a light; when, however, it is heated up between 200 and 300°, it easily inflames, and burns with a very bright and smoky flame. Although it gives off but little vapour, its odour is strong, and exactly similar to ordinary Persian naphtha; and, in fact, it agrees with that substance in all points but two. These are, first, its density is greater; and, secondly, its tendency to congeal or solidify is greater. The cause of these peculi-

brain, and is made to exude by hanging him up by the heels over a slow fire. It is much valued; a great deal is brought from Kabul, but that from Little Tibet is preferred. I presented some of it to Runjit Sing, and he seemed to prize it highly. Marvellous are the stories related of the cures it will perform, in cases of fracture; but, without

arities is, that the naphtha holds in solution a fixed bituminous substance, which is considerably heavier than naphtha, and which is solid in common temperature. When the crude naphtha is submitted to careful distillation, there first comes over a small portion of water, to the presence of which the turbidness of the liquid is due; the liquid in the retort then begins to boil, and the pure naphtha passes over, the boiling point rising all the time, until at last there remains a dark-coloured, almost opaque, pitch-like matter, which becomes solid as it cools. By rectifying the distilled naphtha several times, I obtained it colourless, and perfectly like common naphtha, but rather more dense, its specific gravity being 0·8168. From all this, it appears that the fluid is naphtha, holding in solution a bituminous matter." This bituminous matter is probably mumiai. Some of it was brought from Kabul by Lieutenant Conolly, and an analysis of it is to be seen in the Journal of the Calcutta Asiatic Society.

believing a tenth part of them, I have heard of some from authorities I cannot doubt. A person having fractured a bone is immediately made to swallow a large pill of mumiai. The dose is repeated in a day or two. Milk is, I believe, his diet thenceforth until the limb is recovering. It must act, I should presume, as a very powerful stimulant, so as to increase the necessary secretions; but, at all events, I am so well assured by every one that the limb is sound again in a very short space of time, that I am almost tempted to believe, with Sancho, that I might safely say I had seen its effects tried myself; which, however, I have not, although I have seen many, particularly in Little Tibet, who professed to have been cured by it. It is the *mumia orientalis* of the ancients; and the Egyptian mummies (whence the name?) were swathed with cloths dipped in mumiai.—*Vide Ure's Dictionary of Chemistry—Asphaltum.*

Whilst remaining at Derabund the mountaineers were constantly worrying the Lohanis, prowling like jackals round the camp after nightfall; and, on the very eve of our departure the alarm drums were beaten, and a party set out to retake thirty camels, which the marauders had surprised, and were driving off to the mountains. They desisted, as the rescue approached. The stoppage of the water-courses was another serious cause of a quarrel. The mountaineers descended in the night, and turned the principal stream by which the camp was supplied. A well-armed party sallied forth, in the morning, to the place where the dam had been made. The mountaineers fled at their approach; and they returned from the expedition, singing, shouting, and dancing a regular war dance, brandishing at the same time their drawn swords. The day of departure was at length fixed; but on the evening before, we heard that some Lohanis had been detained by the Nawab of Dhera Ismael Khan, and their relatives went round the camp with the Koran in their hand, praying their friends, for the love of God and respect for the true faith, to remain one day longer, and give the detenus a chance of recovering their liberty; which, on the morrow, I was glad to hear they had purchased for two thousand rupees.

MARKHUR GOAT.

CHAPTER III.

The Kafila—The Caravan sets out—High Temperature—Ladies mounted on Camels—Their Dress—The order maintained—Night Guards—Zurkhaneh—Shonkul—Great height of the Thermometer—Gomul River—Medical practice—Encamp at Monjighurra—Tax levied here—Mountaineer ferocity—Enter the Territory of the Tak Rajah—Alarm of Attack—Mountain Strata—Nilei—Enter a Defile—The Vuziris—Precaution taken—Lohani Graves—The Serpent-eater—Ursak—The Tukt-i-Suliman—Fresh Alarm—Reach Terapore—Treatment of a Sick Man—Scuffle with a Holy Man—A Lohani Funeral—Predestination.

THE kafila, or caravan, in which I travelled, is the last and the largest of those that pro-

F 2

ceed every year from Derabund to Kabul. The first and second start nearly on the same day. A person wishing to travel with the first, should calculate upon arriving at Derabund before the tenth of April; if with the second, before the twentieth or twenty-fifth of the same month; the third or largest is more uncertain, but its day of departure is usually the tenth or twelfth of May. The first kafila carries with it the coarse goods of Moghiana (a town situated on the Chenab river), and the salt of the Punjab. The whole of these goods are disposed of at Ghuzni, Kabul, and Kandahar. The camels of the second kafila are burdened with indigo, purchased at Multan and Buhawulpore, and the chintz of Hindustan. Some part of this investment finds its way to Bokhara. The third, which is the largest, consists of the Lohanis Sirdagur, who cannot exactly time their arrival, as they travel from Hydrabad, Calcutta, Benares, Delhi, Jypore, and the other large cities of India. The bulk of their lading consists of kimkab or golden cloth of Benares, English chintzes and calicos, gun-locks, and similar articles. A great proportion of these goods is transported beyond the Hindu Kosh. The last and longest of the Lohanis kafilas moved back this year from Ghuzni towards Derabund, on the fifteenth of October. They carry pomegranates, almonds, raisins, and ruwash, from Kabul; and from Bokhara, horses, cochineal, nankin, gold thread, raw silk, and other goods. The Emperor Baber cursorily mentions the Lohanis several times, in his memoirs. He appears to have considered and treated them as natives of Hindustan, who were opposed to the progress of his arms in that country. They traded then as now, and their merchandise was of the same description. Ferishta mentions that Bahadur Khan, son of Duria Khan Lohani, governor of Behar, assumed the title of king, under the name of Mohamed Shah, and found himself, shortly before his master Ibrahim was defeated by Baber at Paniput, at the head of one hundred thousand rebel horse, and that he beat the Delhi (Ibrahim's) troops in several engagements. I do not find him mentioned in Baber. Besides the Lohanis, there are five or six kafilas which annually pass the Hindu Kosh for Bokhara, laden with various wares. We marched on the nineteenth of May, and encamped under some trees, at a place called Lalukote. Up to the eighth or twelfth, the weather had been tolerable; on that day the thermometer stood at ninety-eight degrees, in the shade of a well-covered mud building. It had risen gradually every day; and on the twentieth, it stood at one hundred and eleven, in the same building, although it was cooled as much as possible by a frequent sprinkling of water on the floor. In the open air, the hot gusts were like the heat of a furnace. I kept off fever by sleeping in the open air, abstemious and regular diet, breakfasting on suji or the heart of wheat, with water; dining on a boiled chicken, or chicken broth; and drinking a very considerable quantity of black tea.

We were now fairly *en route;* and, considering all things, it was surprising how little confusion there was. About two hours before daylight, the whole kafila was in motion, preceded by a few straggling matchlock men, and a drummer to beat the alarm. Then followed the numerous camels, laden and unladen. The ladies of the Zunanas rode upon a kind of square platform, composed of innumerable cushions; at each corner arose a small tower of the same formation; protected and supported by these, they seemed to be exceedingly comfortable. Chocolate, trimmed with a little yellow, was the predominant colour worn; and the whole turn out, the camels included, was ornamented with fringes and devices, made of cowrie shells. The shyness with which the ladies at first regarded the Feringi, now wore off a little; and they often seemed careless of being observed, covering their faces but very scantily. Some of them were exceedingly handsome; usually very fair, with regular features, black hair, eyes hazel, and blackened eyelids. The young girls wore a single braid in front, which supported a piece of gold, a coin, or other ornament, dangling between the eyes. The married women wore massive gold earrings, composed of thin plates, strung together. Children were perched in every place, and in every attitude; most of them had an unhealthy look, and bad eyes, arising from the enormous quantity of grease and sweetmeats they were allowed to eat; they resembled puppets, and wore caps, shaped like those of a Spanish inquisitor. The cavaliers pranced along gallantly by the side of their ladies, usually riding on mares, as horses would be incessantly fighting. I was myself obliged to change my English curb and snaffle for a "Regulus" bit, studded with blunted spikes. The composure with which the horse, a very spirited animal that Runjit had presented to me, conducted himself afterwards, was surprising; whereas, before, it was a service of constant danger to myself and others to ride him. Herds of cattle, of the half-bred humped breed, light, active, and not easily fatigued by wading through streams, and treading over rocks, were mixed up with goats and sheep, that were threading their way amongst the larger animals. An ass of Bokhara, the only one of the caravan, attracted my attention; it was white, and a very noble animal, much larger than any I had ever seen before.

The price at Bokhara was about sixty Kabul rupees, or four pounds sterling.

I am not aware of a caravan in any eastern country where the manners of a Mussulman family can be so well observed; nor do I think there is any place, where the Mahometan women of rank appear so much in public. Upon arriving at our ground, it was always surprising to observe the celerity with which the camels were unladen. The burdens were piled up like a wall, on the western side of the tent, so that the owners' heads might rest against it, in the direction of the prophet's tomb, at Mecca. The tent, or rather a dark brown pall, was then pitched, generally by the ladies, and in ten minutes all was ready; a short meal, and a long siesta followed; and for three or four hours the whole camp was so hushed, that had it not been for the eternal braying of the sleepless donkey, I should not have been aware of its existence. In the afternoon, every one was awake; the camels were driven in by the watchmen; the men seated themselves in groups, to smoke and chat; women gossipped from tent to tent; and the children were enjoying the inexpressible pleasure of making a noise. The evening meal was then prepared, and the tents struck, before they retired to rest, so that there might be no delay in the morning. The guards loudly challenged throughout the whole of the night, firing their matchlocks, whenever they thought prowlers were at hand. The next morning, not more than a quarter of an hour elapsed, between the commencement of the bustle, and the general move forward.

Zurkhaneh was the next station. The march was a short one, but with little shade. The Nawab takes two thousand rupees yearly from the sheik of this district. The next march was of sixteen miles, to Shonkul, a station bare of trees, and where the mercury rose to one hundred and eighteen degrees in my tent. There the Lohanis hailed with joy the stream of the Gomul, from which we drank; it came, they said, from Belat, four days' march this side of Ghuzni.

I was getting into great reputation by the distribution of medicine. A few days before, I had saved the life of one of the principal Lohanis, who was dangerously ill with dysentery. My next patient was a young lady, from one of their Zunanas, veiled of course, and in company with other women; but I saw all the lower part of a very pretty face, by assuring her it was quite necessary to see her tongue. I made her uncover both her arms, which were richly ornamented, by expressing a serious anxiety to ascertain the state of both pulses. I advised on her case, and, I suppose, successfully, as she did not visit me again.

Our line of march now lay to the north-west, following the course of the stream; and the caravan encamped at Manjighurra. From this place, the Tukt-i-Suliman bore south-south-west. The town of Derabund was in the south-east. Dhera Ismael Khan, and the hills of Karabagh, lay to the eastward. The town of Tâk, the residence of a Rajah, or Nawab, is situated in the plain, about fifteen or twenty miles to the northward. The Lohanis told me, he received a tax of two rupees, from every laden camel, and that his family were originally Lohani. He was then said to purchase exemption from trouble, on this side the Attok, by paying yearly, a sum of several thousand rupees, to Runjit Sing, but his dominions were invaded shortly afterwards; he fled from the superior power of the Sikhs, and when I was at Kabul, he came in person before Dost Mahomed, sitting in full durbar, to throw himself and his family on his protection. I had not believed all the stories I had heard of the bold ferocity of the Vuziri Paharis, or mountaineers. Ameer Khan would never allow me to move from the camp, even for a few yards, as night drew near. At this place, two men, who had been lying a little away from the edge of the crowd, were killed with swords in the night; one, whilst he was asleep, and the other for crying out, and giving the alarm. The feeling of hostility against the Lohanis had its origin, in their refusing to pay any thing for permission to pass through the mountains. I think the demands of the mountaineers are justifiable, as the Lohanis pay permit money in every other country they pass through, from Calcutta to St. Macaire, or Makari, as they term it, on the frontiers of Russia. The consequence of their withholding it, is a bloody feud, producing robbery and vexation. I used to tell Ameer Khan, and the other Lohanis, they were wrong not to make an arrangement, and pay some trifle, however small, and I am not sure they were not of my opinion, although they did not say so, merely remarking, that it would be of no use, and that the depredations would still be continued.

The next day we made a short march into the territories of the Tâk Rajah, and an hour or two afterwards arrived at the foot of the hills, the entrance to them being in full view. Suddenly the alarm was given, and the fighting men of the Kafila went forward, under a terrific heat, to take possession of a gorge in the mountains, to where marauders, who had been watching the opportunity, had driven off some camels. They returned at night, with the loss of five, and two men wounded. I now found that events of this kind were of daily occurrence. The next morning, to my great joy, for I was much weakened by the heat, we fairly entered the hills, by a low pass, formed entirely, as indeed the country had been for three days past, of hardened shingle, and disturbed strata, rising at every quarter and at every angle. The three last changes that have taken place in the surface of the country were easily remarked. The lowest stratum, of mountain lime-stone, was so arched and contorted, that it must have been subjected to more than one convulsion. The shingly deposit that covered this stratum, was not raised with the lime-stone, as it no where yielded to its configuration. Whenever the shingle was seen on the mountains, in the interior, it lay in denuded and horizontal strata, so that the low, broken, and confused masses which skirt the plain, and have no visible substratum of limestone, must have been shaken into their present position by subsequent convulsions, causing them to sink from their original level. No man in his senses can deny that these had once been covered by the sea. Every pebble in the country was rounded by the action of water; and remnants of marine shells, and a vast profusion of Ammonites and Nummullites, were scattered over the encamping ground. The next day's march was to Rylu, and we halted on an open plain, apart from the river. The water we drank was brackish, brought from a spring at the foot of the mountain, on the east side. The space around the spring was described to me as being almost covered with fragments of shells and marine remains. My servants brought me some specimens, similar to those I had picked up the day before.

The mountain summit appeared to be composed of greyish limestone; on the bank below it there was chalk; and beneath that I think there was a bed of marl. I regretted very much that the intense heat prevented my going there myself, as in all probability I should have found fossil remains.

On the thirtieth we marched for several miles through a defile formed by perpendicular walls of shingle, varying in height from fifty feet to two hundred, and in width from twenty to three hundred yards. This spot is a favourite haunt of the Vuziri robbers, as the caravan is necessarily much exposed and the cavalry is unable to act. A gorge which opens into the defile was described to me as the scene of an action three years before. Nine hundred robbers made their appearance, cut off the leading camels, and drove them to the mountain, but they were recovered after two days' fighting. The Kafila did not now entirely escape. Three good men, and true, who were escorting the last of the caravan, were shot in the back, after passing an ambuscade, but were carried off by their friends. They died before night; their horses, which were of value, and a few camels with them, were taken away by the robbers.

"The Vuziris," Mr. Moorcroft has remarked before, "are 'nomades.' If they have any villages or fixed habitations they are certainly not near the road of the Lohanis, who would soon attack and destroy them. Might not the word 'numud,' or 'felt,' of which the tents of the wandering tribes of Asia have always been and still are composed, have supplied the root to the word *νομαδικος*, instead of the word *νεμω* to feed, as given by Johnson?"

We halted a day in the defile, in order

to bury our unfortunate Lohani. A council of war was held, and it was judged expedient, for fear of the mountaineers, that the caravan should be divided into two parts, and that one should march two days before the other; by this means, the confusion that would arise in case of another attack on such a dense crowd might be avoided. Lots were drawn by the principal Lohanis, and it was decided that we should march first; but so numerous was the caravan, that there did not appear any difference, in point of numbers, then or before.

On the first of June we encamped at Shydan, by the river side. During the two last days water had only been procured by scraping away the ground, and had been alike scarce, brackish, and unwholesome. On the way to Koteghye, the next day, we passed the scene of a battle that took place some fifty years ago: the Vuziri mountaineers came down in such force upon the Lohanis, that it was deemed prudent to listen to their demands. A certain sum was to be paid to them at a distance from the camp; a scramble ensued for the rupees, and those who got none insisted upon more being paid them. A fight was the consequence, which ended in favour of the Lohanis; but a considerable loss of lives on both sides took place. A pile of stones covers the Lohanis' graves, and a wall of the same material surrounds them. Sticks are inserted amongst the stones, and upon these are generally put the offerings of their friends, in the shape of wreaths and pieces of cloth. The horns of the moufflon, or wild sheep, called here the "koch," were intermixed with those of the ibex or chup, and the markhur or rawacheh of Little Tibet described hereafter. We passed burial-places for many days successively, and their appearance was melancholy and desolate in the extreme. Some peaceable Vuziris from a neighbouring village came into the camp, and from them I procured a good skin of the markhur, or serpent-eater. I was assured that this animal, which was a gigantic goat, had a penchant for eating snakes; seizing them by the tail, and swallowing them. I tell the tale as it was seriously told to me, without vouching for the truth of it. I was delighted to find the horns of this animal, of which I had never before seen or heard. When I was at Kabul, Mohamed Akber Khan, the second son of Dost Mohamed Khan, who was out on an expedition in Lughman, killed one in the mountains and sent it to me.

Its length, from the nose to the tip of the tail, was five feet eight inches; it was, I was assured, by no means a large one; the height, at the shoulder, was three feet three inches; round the fore-arm, eleven inches; its legs being very short and thick. The circumference of its fore-foot was nearly eleven inches; its massive horns were thirty-one and a half inches in length, lyral in their general outline, but having two spiral curves between the roots and the point. It had five grinders in each jaw, and eight front-teeth in the lower jaw. It had no suborbital sinus, which the ibex has. I should place it as the link between the ibex and the common goat, which it more resembles than any animal I know. In Greece, where the goats' horns are very large, I have seen some that closely resembled those of the markhur, excepting in size. The colour of this goat is rufous brown, generally; its head more of a chocolate colour; its beard, which is very long and extends from the chin to the breast, is a clear yellowish white; tail black; rump and legs, downwards, hocks and knees included, dirty white; black over the rump and hocks; and a black stripe, gradually lessening, passing from behind each knee to the front of the fetlock joint. It is common in Little Tibet and the higher mountain country lying between the Indus, Budukshan, and the Hindu Kosh. In Little Tibet it is seen on inaccessible precipices, of little elevation, overhanging the river.

On the third of June we crossed the stream of the river at least fifty times on the way to Kangur, an open space, on which arose a lofty bank of alluvium. The mountains are formed of schist and limestone; the strata lying at every angle, and often capped with shingly deposit. Still following up the course of the river, on the fourth of June we encamped at Ursuk. From this place the Tukt-i-Suliman was visible to the east-south-east. Information had been given that some thieves had descended into the neighbouring plain. A strong party of Lohanis mounted in the heat of the day, but returned soon, saying it had been a false alarm. In the afternoon a grass-cutter, who had wandered too far, returned to the camp; he had been seized and frightened by fifteen Vuziris, who told him that they were all concealed on the ground when the Lohanis passed within a quarter of a mile of them. Their feelings must have been agreeable, knowing that they would all inevitably have been put to death, had they been discovered. The grass-cutter had escaped from them, merely on account of his low office. A Lohani of rank would have been their victim.

On the fifth of June we reached Terapore. The mountain of Marawallah, celebrated as the nursery of the Byri, or peregrine falcon, bore about north-east.

The thermometer stood at one hundred and four in my tent; but even this was a grateful difference. The mornings and evenings were becoming cold. I was awakened at night by the cautionary uproar from the firing of the matchlocks, and a false alarm of thieves; and I listened with sorrow to the wailings of the women, proceeding from a neighbouring tent, as I knew that a death which I had foretold had taken place there. About ten days before, I had been requested to attend upon a sick Lohani, a near relation of Ameer Khan. He was a young man, tall, stout, and very fat. I found that he had had fever for two days; his eyes were starting from his temples, and his cheeks swollen and flushed. I gave him some medicine; and, the next day, had him bled in the hand by a native practitioner. Even this was only allowed by my most earnest entreaties. A prayer was said by the friends who surrounded his bed, before the vein was opened, and a small cupfull of blood was all they would allow to be taken; Ameer Khan holding his other pulse whilst the operation was going on, and expressing his surprise and pleasure at the sudden alteration for the better. The invalid, finding immediate relief, sat up in bed, and swore that he must eat something directly, or that he should die from starvation, having eaten nothing for two days. I was obliged to allow him some broth, and I believe he ate a great deal more when I was absent. I was astonished at the little idea these people had of keeping an invalid quiet. I sent his friends away several times from his bed; but immediately as my back was from them, they returned like bees to a hive. Each seized a limb, which they immediately began to mull,—that is, to pinch with the whole hand, from one extremity to the other; another sat at his head, and began the same operation on his temples; in fact, the poor man stood a good chance of being smothered. I was one day obliged to hand outside of my tent-ropes, by force, a conceited, simpering, young Syud, a descendant of the Prophet, who would persist in sitting by the invalid's bed, afterI had civilly requested him to depart five times. Unaccustomed to such treatment,—for he was a holy man, which luckily I did not know,—he turned pale with fear and passion; and, grasping a handful of stones and sand, was going to throw them at me, muttering with a choked voice, in Persian, "Now, I will kill you, you Infidel." It was lucky he was not armed. He walked off in a rage; and I retired into my tent, with my shirt-sleeve torn in the scuffle. The affair was amicably settled by Ameer Khan, on the understanding that I did not know him to be a holy man. Meanwhile, in spite of my entreaties, they still persisted in feeding my patient; and, consequently, there was a great increase of fever. All my remonstrances were of no use; they would not again allow me to bleed him. Scraps of the Koran were tied around the sick man's neck. One fellow was for giving him a fish sherbet, by way of something very cooling; another called for a cup of cold water, and, having muttered a prayer over it, held it close to the sick man's face, and blew over it precisely as a conjuror does when he says, "*Presto,*—be gone." Another passed a lighted piece of paper, on which was written a verse of the Koran, around his head, and held it smoking under his nose; this, of course, had much the same effect as a cup of salt-and-water. Inquiring friends never thought of putting a question to any one but the invalid himself; who the day before he died, answered that he was much better. In spite of all the mistaken kindness of his friends, the intense heat, and the daily risk of increase of fever on the march, I for the time again procured him a cool head, a clean tongue, and a good pulse; and only requested that he might be brought every day to my tent, as the quietest place in the camp. His friends, however, were so desperately afraid that I should take more blood from him, or compel him to take more medicine, that they kept him in their own tents, refusing him nothing he asked. His fever again returned; and on the next day, at his own request, they adopted the very primitive treatment of wrapping him in a wet cloth, from head to foot, with a strong, hot wind blowing upon him. At night he was gasping from inflammation, and to bleed him to the extent that was necessary was quite out of the question. I procured him some repose by a powerful dose of medicine, and putting his feet in hot water; to prepare which, my servants and self were disturbed three times in one night. All entreaties and expostulations were vain; the next day I saw the wet sheet around him again. He then felt himself sinking, just as we were only a few days' march from the cool air of Khorassan. He now sent for me, and presented me with a small flower, adding that it was of Khorassan, that the air and the water there were cool, and that he had again hoped to see it. His hand was like ice. Ameer Khan said, "that now he was better." I took Ameer aside, and told him he could not live above five or six hours; at which he seemed shocked. The poor fellow died in the night, as I had foretold, and was buried at the next station. His friends carried his body on a chaharpase, or "four feet" (a bedstead). On the road, the day before he died, we passed the grave of a Lohani of rank; they bore the body up to it, muttered a hasty prayer to the departed saint, and pushed forward. He was buried at Semla Borag, the next station, completely sacrificed to the bo ok-bound ignorance of Mahometanism. His friends buried him on a bleak and barren mountain-desert; a heap of stones his only monument; the wild goat's horn his only epitaph; and the murmuring of the Gomul his only requiem. No vestige of a habitation was near him. His grave designates the place to the eastward of which the snows of Afghanistan are rarely known to fall.

Thanks to the doctrine of predestination, and the name of an Englishman, I was under no alarm on the score of being accused of accelerating his death by my treatment. "It would have been all the same," said Ameer Khan, "had the first doctor in Hindustan been here; it was his fate, and God so willed it, and nothing would have saved him. The most eminent

Christian divines have disputed, and will dispute, on predestination. Mahomed has contrived to entice half the world into a belief of it; and yet a Mahomedan, fighting against the Infidels, must either feel assured that he is pleasing the Prophet, without any chance of his fate being the better for it; or must be contradicting his own creed, by inconsistently thinking that a meritorious death will be of service to him in after-life. Mahomed has made use of the doctrine for the spreading of his own opinions; and has neutralized all the revolting and disagreeable part of it, by allowing his followers a life of sensuality, and the prospect of a heaven, than which the warmest imagination cannot paint one more likely to attract converts. I look upon a Mussulman, who fully believes that he is predestinated to a place in the Prophet's paradise, as rather an enviable person than otherwise.

THE LOHANI'S GRAVE.

CHAPTER IV

Arrival at Karandur—Sirmagha—Vegetable Soap—Edible Rhubarb—Parting for Kandahar of some of the Lohanis—Encamp in a Mountain Pass—Scenery and Delicious Breeze—Thermometer and Elevation—Suliman Kyl Tribe—Mode of Robbing—Tribute to Dost Mahomed Khan—Boundaries—Encamp at Katawaz—Dsharah Ridge—Mountain Sheep—Ruins of Zohaka—Sand Grouse—Eyesight Judgment of the Aborigines—Round Forts—Revenue-Officers from Kabul—Ameer Khan's Killah—Illness of the Author—Proceed to Ghuzni—Character of the Lohanis—Scenery around Ghuzni.

On the fifteenth of June we arrived at Sturei, and, on the sixteenth, at Karandur, both on the same stream. Whilst we were nearer the plains, the boys used to catch a fish, which I believe to be the Mahasir of the Indian waters; but to-day I saw them catch another kind of fish, such as is found in Kashmir and in all the streams on the south side of the Himalaya. It is described in the Journal of Asiatic Society of Bengal, for January 1835, p. 39. The fish I allude to is certainly not a trout, as it has a valved mouth.

A species of cicada was swarming upon every scanty leaf and blade of grass. These insects were eagerly seized by the pedestrians; first spitted, then roasted, and afterwards eaten in scores.

The dreary barrenness of the lower range began now to diminish; and tufts of grass, wild tulips, and aromatic plants were spread over the hills. At Sirmagha, the next day's station, the Lohanis began every where to dig up a ligneous root, containing a saponaceous kernel, with which they washed their clothes. Shortly before reaching Dormundai, an open airy station where we encamped on the tenth of June, the ground was joined by another stream, called the Shei Gomul,—Shei in Poshtu, the language of Afghanistan, signifying the right; and the old stream, whose course we still followed up, being called the Kena, or left Gomul. The aromatic plants here were very numerous; the wild onion and caraway plant were in great abundance. I dug up several specimens of the Ruwand chini, a native species of edible rhubarb, distinct however from the celebrated Ruwash of Kabul. I have long supposed the silphium of Arrian to be the prangus of Mr. Moorcroft. At least, I know of nothing else that is so husbanded as food for cattle, excepting perhaps the willow leaves in

Kashmir. It is in favour of this theory, that the prangus was well known to the ancients as a gigantic species of parsley. I have seen it growing at a height of six thousand feet in Kashmir, and in ranges between that and eight thousand feet. I find that Dr. Royle is of the same opinion. He informs me, that the seed of the prangus (prangus pabularia) is brought down by the northern merchants, and sold in the bazaars of northern India, under the name of "Fiturasalyon," to which name, in Persian works, is attached a translation of the description of the Petroselinon, (πετροσέλινον or rock parsley).—Diosc. lib. iii. c. 77. Mr. Masson, I think, told me that he imagined the silphium to have been the scented wormwood (artemisia), which is so common throughout the East. As I was speaking of different plants, I mention the prangus, but I did not find it on the Suliman range; though perhaps it may exist there.

The rear kafila came up with us on the eleventh, when we passed some barley-fields and a small fort constructed by Barbuk Khan, Zemindar, or chief of the soil in these parts. From this place, part of the caravan took the road to Kandahar westward, which they expected to reach in ten days. We followed up the stream to the north, and encamped about three miles beyond the fort. A large town called Urghun, filled with iron-manufactories, and subjected to Dost Mahomed Khan, lay about two marches to the north-west of us. The inhabitants of this part of the country are called Karati.

On the twelfth of June we made the last ascent, and encamped on the Sir-i-koh or head of the mountain, being the highest part of the pass between Derabund and Ghuzni. Ledges of fine sand-stone rose above the summits and sides of the mountains. These last were broken and tumbled about like the waves of the sea. The air was perfumed with aromatic plants. A few trees were scattered here and there, chiefly wild-olives and mountain-ash. Such was the scenery on the ascent. A delicious breeze was blowing from the north, when a Patan gallopped by me, exclaiming "Khorassan! Khorassan!" and adding, "Sahib! Sahib! a breath of this would be worth a lak of rupees in Hindustan." I quite agreed with him.

We then saw the last of the Gomul river, a mere streamlet. I passed over the summit of the hill, and drank, delighted, of the stream that flowed downwards to the west. "Khorassan! Khorassan!" was the cry, and every one in the caravan seemed to be aware, that the prospect of that country was at hand. I should remark, that the Lohanis do not, in speaking of

Khorassan, confine their meaning to Khorassan proper, but extend the appellation, as in Baber's time, up to the western foot of the Sulimani mountains.

The first and most prominent object was the range of Narawah on the north-west, with snow on its summits. The direction of Ghuzni and Kabul was to the west. Kandahar lay west by south, and the Tukt-i-Suliman and Derabund lay to the south-east. It seemed as if a day's march were sufficient to bring us to the plain of Ghuzni; and beyond it numerous low ranges of hills conducted the eye to the western horizon. The thermometer, at mid-day, stood at eighty-four in the shade; its boiling-point gave an elevation of about eight thousand feet.

An alarm was given towards evening, that some camels had been driven off;

their keepers were telegraphing their information, by hurling dust into the air from the top of the distant hill. The Lohanis gave chase; and the robbers escaped, leaving the animals to be taken possession of by their owners.

A tribe called the Suliman Kyl occupied the district which we were entering, which ranges from north to south on the Ghuzni side of the pass. There are said to be about twelve thousand of them, nearly all thieves, but not so bloodthirsty or formidable as the Vuziris of the mountains near Derabund. They will not kill a man in cool blood without reason; and their attacks rather resemble those made by the nightly prowlers of India, who creep into your house or tent, and steal a ring from your finger, or take a sheet from under you, without waking you. Some of the Suliman Kyl confessed to a Lohani whom they knew, that they were prowling about my tent all night, but that the watchmen were too much on the alert; adding, that they thought it meritorius to rob a Feringi; and that to have killed me an infidel, if necessary, would have been a sure passport to heaven.

They will combine together to resist any thing like a serious invasion. Fourteen years ago, Jumar Khan, a Durani of rank, was sent from Kabul by Azim Khan, having four thousand men, and two cannon, with instructions to reduce a fort belonging to Taj Khan, one of their refractory chiefs; but the Suliman Kyl attacked him in the night with superior numbers, and succeeded in killing or dispersing the whole of his force; he himself losing his life in the action. The Suliman Kyl were in possession, I was told, of a million of sheep, and they paid a yearly tribute of one camel, for every forty men, to Dost Mahomed Khan. Their country extends from north to south, for seven or eight caravan-marches, between Ghuzni and Kandahar, and for two or three from east to west. Once a year, in the winter season, they send a kafila of three or four hundred camels into the plains of Derabund, and Dhera Ismael Khan. They are chiefly laden with madder-roots; and with the produce of this, they purchase a sufficient quantity of the coarse cloths of the Punjab, as a supply for the whole of their tribe. They remain about twenty days in the plains, and then retire to their country by the same route.

The Ruwash of Kabul is common on this side of the hill; several leaves of it were brought to me.

The next morning we descended gently towards the west, and encamped on a sloping plain at a place called Shintzah. A mud fort belonging to a Zemindar was seen in the distance to the west; and on the fourteenth, we pitched at Katawaz, on the plains of the Suliman Kyl.

Between the Sir-i-koh, or summit of the pass, which we had left some days back, and the Dsharah ridge, which we were approaching, there might be a distance of from twenty to twenty-five miles. Here and there was a little wheat, which I was assured had been in the ground nearly a twelvemonth already, as it had been sown before the first snow fell in the preceding year. The plain in general was covered with sand, and glittering with innumerable and most minute particles of crystal; and here and there were patches of wild-thyme, which imparted a delicious fragrance to the air. Many of the Suliman Kyl were prowling through the camp; a wild, and impudent-looking set of fellows: some selling sheep and grass, were well contented, after having made a good bargain; and others were made happy by the pacifying present of a new turban. The sheep of this district are the Dumbi, or large-tailed sheep of Persia, with long ears, a small, plump, and very good-looking animal, of a dark reddish brown colour.

Numerous mud forts, each I believe containing a small village, were scattered over the plain before us.

On the continuation of the even-topped ridge of the Sir-i-koh, are to be seen, as I was informed, the ruins of a large city, called Zohaka[1], after a king who reigned there, before the time of the Mussulmen. Three gates of burnt brick are still standing, and I was told, there was a deep

[1] See note at the end.

pool there, the water of which, so tradition affirmed, finds its way to the Indus by a subterraneous channel. Altogether, in the country around, there was much that reminded me of Persia; the cool air, scented with artemisia or wormwood, and wild-thyme; the walled gardens of mulberry and apricot trees; the long Kanaats or covered water-courses, and the gurgling cry of the bovra korra (black breast), or large sand grouse, which we frequently disturbed. These birds afforded me good sport, to the delight of the Lohanis, many of whom had never seen any thing killed with shot before. In Poshtu, the birds are termed the Tuturuk, which name well expresses their call. The Lohanis amused themselves by galloping after the antelope, which appeared to me, in the distance, to resemble the common antelope of Hindustan.

It seemed that the Suliman Kyl are too formidable to be displeased or slighted; and the caravan halted the next day, when the propriety of their demands for black mail was amicably discussed, and the rate of payment settled. These uneducated Aborigines are dependent on their eye-sight for suggestion, to an extent that is hardly credible; a man has only to appear poor, and they believe that he is so. Ameer Khan would not allow me to have my tent pitched, and I lay the whole day under an old pall, that had been torn by the donkeys and camels running against the ropes. Many of the Suliman Kyl passed around my tent, looking exceedingly inquisitive, and exclaiming at first that my packages were filled with rupees; however, I escaped with apparently little notice, and the payment of a very small sum.

On the sixteenth of June, we marched

on the Dsharah hills, which were open, gently undulating, and covered with soil. Here and there appeared small peaks of limestone, and denuded masses of hardened shingle; and occasionally on the plain lay, with no rock of the kind near it, a large accidental block of limestone, which had been projected from a distance, or left there by the waters of the deluge.

The plain into which we descended, on the seventeenth, extended to the foot of the Narawah mountains, which lay before us. On the north-west, I should think, that the hill over which we had just passed was, if my thermometer can be trusted, a few hundred feet lower than the Sir-i-koh. The plain was studded with neat-looking mud forts, which evinced an assumption of independence on the part of his subjects, telling ill for the stability of Dost Mahomed Khan's power. In the night, before the alarm could be given, some thieves crept into a tent, and carried away a quantity of linen. At this place, some of Dost Mahomed's revenue-officers arrived from Kabul; and it was found necessary to halt a day, in order to enable them to finish their arrangements.

On the morning of the nineteenth of June, the caravan might be seen dividing, each party making for a separate village or fort, with the intention of remaining there a few days, weeks, or even months, according to the time required for the sale of their merchandise to the wild inhabitants of the numerous forts on the plain, and the still wilder Hazarah tribes, who descend from the snowy range of the Narawah mountains, for the purpose of traffic. These people are said to affirm that they, and the Ghorkas of Nipal, are descended from one stock: a few of them visited our encampment, and their features did not belie their assertion. They, as well as the Undas or natives of the country, were clad with coats made of sheep-skins. They appeared to be larger men, and, as mountaineers, seemed to be much more oppressed with the heat of the plains, than the Ghorkas, but they had the same small eyes, high cheek-bones, and flattened noses, entirely different from the Undas, who were generally fair, and with rather good features. I afterwards saw many of them, and found that a large proportion of the population of Ghuzni were Hazarahs.

We had now arrived at what Ameer Khan called his killah, or castle: it was merely a collection of low mud walls, without a single roof; and along and against these they pitched their tents. I had been led to believe that the caravan itself would proceed to Ghuzni, and that I should see that place in their company. I was much annoyed and surprised by Ameer Khan suddenly telling me that we should remain where we were for a few days, and then proceed to Kabul, without going to Ghuzni. I felt the more hurt at this piece of duplicity on the part of the Lohanis, because I had enjoyed their protection, and had been on the best possible terms with them. It was quite evident, that kind as they had been, they were acting as all Mussulmen will, from interested motives; though I by no means wish to say, that they were actuated by them alone; as I repeat, that I received the greatest kindness at their hands, and felt, and still do feel, grateful for their protection; but it was necessary to see such a place as Ghuzni. I had, some eight days before, sent forward a note to the Nawab, Jabar Khan, brother of Dost Mahomed Khan, whose son Abdul Ghias Khan had written to him about me from Lodiana, so that I expected a man to be sent to me from him. The Lohanis were now guilty of wilful misrepresentation, and objected to my going to Ghuzni, telling me I should be robbed and plundered by the young Sirdar, a son of Dost Mahomed, who was then in command; that their caravan would march forward in three days, and in fact saying every thing they could think of to prevent my going. I was all this time lying unwell in my tent, having been fairly poisoned by the bad water I had drunk during the march. I was so ill, that I thought it necessary to apply leeches to my chest. There were plenty in the ditches around, but I found, on the application of them, that they were utterly useless. Altogether I was glad, one day, to observe a Sewar or horseman riding into the camp, and making for my tent; his name was Mortazu Khan; he was an old servant of the Nawab's, and the head of a Kuzzelbash family, that had the care of their master's camels, on an estate situated at Khargh, a long day's march in the Hazarah mountains. He had received orders to attend on me, wherever I chose to roam, and to summon as many more of his clansmen as I wished, to act as mounted guards. My Lohani friends tried to talk him over; but I rode forward to Ghuzni the next day. I left them in very bad health, and somewhat out of humour. The fact was, they wished to detain me, that I might go with them to Kabul. They would have made fifty different uses of the name of a Feringi; and to have brought and protected me throughout their whole march, and to have accompanied me to the presence of the Nawab, would, they imagined, have gained them favour in the eyes of the Ameer; and right glad should I have been to have said all I could for them, when the day of their taxation arrived. In fact, we became the best friends afterwards at Kabul, and I did say all I could in their favour.

Taking them altogether, I look upon the Lohanis as the most respectable of the Mahomedans, and the most worthy of the notice and assistance of our countrymen. The Turkish gentleman is said to be a man of his word; he must be an enviable exception; but I otherwise solemnly believe there is not a Mahomedan,—Suni, or Shiah,—between Constantinople and Yarkund, who would hesitate to cheat a Feringi Frank, or European, and who would not lie, and scheme, and try to deceive, when the temptation was worth his doing so, and the contemplated risks of detection were neither prominent, numerous, nor soon to be apprehended. Honesty and fidelity, from interested motives, are common enough; but I appeal to any man who has been in India, to decide whether,—

supposing it were possible that he could send the King of Delhi—the Great Mogul himself—into the bazaar, with a rupee, and a commission to make a purchase,—he would not retain some half-pence for himself, and hand over false change to his employer. All ranks in the East are distinguished, more or less, by an utter want of principle. An honest man is positively stared at as a fool; and detected rascality is accompanied with such an extraordinary power of prevarication, that you are obliged to laugh when you are most willing to be angry. But forgiveness is a galling office, when you are sure there is no repentance from the heart, and that the culprit would repeat the offence when an opportunity was offered, and is—

> "E'en in penance planning sins anew."
>
> *Goldsmith's "Traveller."*

If we consider, that in the time of our Saviour the natives of the East were at least as wicked as at present, divine indeed must shine forth that precept of Christianity, which acknowledges no grade of exasperation, and making neither exception nor compromise, spurns fearlessly the spirit of revenge, and the chances of repetition, and collecting every offence, upon the principle of our own need of it, within the pale of mercy, commands us to forgive even until seventy times seven.

I was now approaching Ghuzni. On the eastern side of the mountains I had traversed with the Lohanis, there was nothing but India. The terrific heat of the day, the barren plain, the furious tufan of the evening, the muddy stream, the scarcity of trees and fruit, the plants, the animals, the natives and their customs, were exclusively Indian. On the western side, at the height of seven thousand feet, I found myself in a totally different climate. There were numerous

On Stone by J. B Pyne from a Drawing by the Author *The Kabul Gate*

VIEW OF GHUZNI

London. Published by Whittaker & Co Ave Maria Lane.

villages, and mud forts standing near every one of them; the glaring sameness of the walls more than relieved by the brilliant green foliage of the fruit-trees that were waving over them. The scented sunjyt,—unknown in India, rare in Kashmir, and common in Persia and Little Tibet,—was growing plentifully amongst the willows on the stream side, and the magpie and the white clover of England were joyfully recognized as old acquaintances. There was much in the prospect to rally and enliven me; and I stood much in need of it, having been a good deal reduced by fever during the preceding fortnight, and my illness had yet scarcely decreased. The Bala Hissar, or fort of Ghuzni, whose summit only was visible over the rise in the plain, soon came entirely in view. The minars, or pillars of Sultan Mahmud, rose majestically to the north of it, on the road to Kabul; and about two miles and a half further, in the same direction, was seen the slope and village-hill of the Ruzeh-i-Sultan, or tomb of the great Mahmud. I believe I may affirm that there is little else to be seen in Ghuzni. The walls of the fort, in the centre of which stands the Bala Hissar, form an irregular pentagon, the sides varying from two to four hundred yards in length. On the west side they are elevated to a height of two hundred and eighty feet above the plain, and the rock might be scarped so as to render it thoroughly inaccessible on that side. The Afghans boast much of the strength of the walls and fortifications of Ghuzni. I thought there were too many towers along them; but these defences, however formidable, would have been of little use in withstanding a regular siege, as I thought (and I am speaking with the greatest deference) that the city could be shelled in some places with tremendous effect from the neighbouring hill I shall hereafter mention; and on which, when I was there, there was no outwork or fortification of any kind whatever. The fortifications were, no doubt, much strengthened by Dost Mahomed Khan, before the arrival of the British force. There are three gates to Ghuzni. One morning I rode into the fort through the Kabul gate: the guards were very civil, but stopped me, saying that it was necessary to have the young Nawab Taj Mahomed Khan's permission. He was outside the city, looking at some cavalry: I turned my horse's head, having merely seen that there was a large open space between the gate and the Bala Hissar. "Kabul is nothing, then!" exclaimed old Mortazu Khan, "and Ghuzni is a great city! Here is the Sahib going to Kabul, and you won't let him see Ghuzni!" and added, with a loud laugh, in ridicule of anything so absurd, "Give me seven or eight hundred men," no disparagement to the late brilliant exploit, "and I'd take this place any day!" "But what are you to do with the walls?" said I. "Oh! of course," he replied, "I mean that I must be inside the walls first." Every Afghan or Patan, when excited in dispute, will boast of a family, an importance, and a number of adherents that he can summon to his aid by the holding up of his finger, which no one ever heard of before; and though, like Owen Glendower, he cannot be pronounced "a worthy gentleman, exceedingly well-read," yet he would—if provoked by a disputant, or encouraged by a good listener—"hold him at least nine hours in reckoning up the several devils' names that were his lackeys." I came away the next day, not choosing to seek an interview with the young Sirdar; having been informed that he was in the habit of asking for your sword, gun, pistol, or anything else to which he might take a fancy.

MAHMUD'S PILLARS.

CHAPTER V.

Ghuzni—Koh-i-Nigar Khaneh Mountains—The Hazarahs—The Fort of Ghuzni—Find one of Mr. Moorcroft's Servants—Sultan Mahmud's Minars—Good offices of the Kuzzelbash—Leave Ghuzni—Bunde-i-Sultan—Baber's Account of Ghuzni—Topes—Visit to a Mine—Chahar Deh—The Nawab's Family—Customs of the Country—Ghilzyes and Dost Mahomed Khan—Military Operations of Dost Mahomed—Attachment of Dost Mahomed to England—Hospitable Reception—Enter Kabul.

GHUZNI is built at the foot of a long narrow ridge of gypsum, generally rounded by the soil that covers it, and in many places split through by the protruding rock[1]. It is projected from the north to the south, and is elevated a few hundred feet above the plain, which extends to the east, west, and south of it. Beyond this, on the west, are the mountains called Koh-i-Nigar Khaneh, or "mountains of the beacons," inhabited (I believe) by Suni Patans. To the south, the plains would seem to reach to Kandahar; and on the west, running from the northern to the southern horizon, are the Hazarah mountains; the snowy peak of the Gul Koh, "the flower mountain," rising conspicuously to the south-south-west. The Hazarahs, who inhabit them, are Shiah

[1] See note at the end.

Mahomedans. The Koh-Haji Lal (if I mistake not the name), or "mountain of the red pilgrim," which I had passed with the Lohanis, bore south-east by south, at a great distance; the Bunde-i-Sultan, which I afterwards visited, lay exactly to the north; and Kabul, to the north-east by north. Within the fort is a moderate bazaar, and at a guess, about a thousand houses, occupied, as I was told, by two thousand Sepahis. I got a glimpse of four guns; one, which, from its size, is called "Zubba-zung," appeared to me to have the bore of a twenty-four-pounder. I was informed two thousand four hundred more Sepahis, horse and foot, were distributed over the country, who pillaged, however, as much as they protected. My tent was pitched close to the Kabul gate, as being the safest place. I was visited by two or three of the principal men of the Nawab's court; more, I believe, to see what baggage I had, than from reasons of courtesy. Mounted Sepahis were constantly passing and repassing to Kabul, where they had been ordered for inspection ; and a wild, ragged crew they were,—Patans, Hindus, Kuzzelbashes ; and a few deserters from the Sikh army, whose services were valuable, as they had been regularly drilled. I found one of Mr. Moorcroft's servants here, in the artillery ; but I could collect nothing from him, but what was already known, respecting that much-regretted traveller, whose name is never mentioned without the greatest respect.

Ghuzni stands, by the thermometer, nearly seven thousand feet above the sea. On the north of the town, about half a mile from the gate, rises the first of Sultan Mahmud's minars, or towers ; the other is about four hundred yards beyond it, in the same direction. They both rise alone, based upon rough stone-work. The most northerly is the handsomest structure, but both are exquisite specimens of brick-work. They are about one hundred and forty feet in height, and much damaged. The section of the lower part of each column, for about one-third of its height, is a star, with, I think, eight points; the upper part is round. They are hollow; and a winding-stair, much damaged, leads to the top. Beautiful ornaments, and inscriptions in Kufic, are placed on different parts of these pillars. Ferishta appears to have been in error; he somewhere says that all the inscriptions at Ghuzni were destroyed. I do not know to what we are to attribute the building of these minars. I could decipher none of the inscriptions; but every one said they were Mahmud's. Perhaps they were part of the great mosque, and they were most likely used by the mullahs when they called to prayers. "The king," says Ferishta, "on his return from Hindustan and the sacking of Mutra, ordered a magnificent mosque to be built of marble and granite, and it was known by the name of 'the celestial bride.' He founded an university near it; and when the nobility of Ghuzni perceived the taste of their king in architecture, they also endeavoured to vie with each other in the magnificence of their private palaces, as well as in public buildings, which were raised for the embellishment of the city. Thus, in a short time, the capital was ornamented with mosques, porches, fountains, reservoirs, aqueducts, and cisterns, beyond any city in the East." The adjoining plain is covered with ruins.

The Ruzu-i-Sultan is placed, as I have remarked, in the midst of a village. A mean entrance, and a plastered Gothic cloister, led to a wretched inner garden, into which open the celebrated sandal-wood gates; within these is the tomb of the once mighty Mahmud. They were, as is well known, brought by him from Somnath in Guzerat,—a temple that was frequented in the time of the eclipses, so says Ferishta, by from two to three hundred thousand people. The idol was supplied twice daily with fresh water from the Ganges, though that river is above a thousand miles distant[1]. The gates have lost their scent from age. The ornaments upon them, many being rosettes, appear to have been exquisitely carved. The tomb is a triangular prism of fine white polished marble, resting on a raised platform of the same material, which they would have me believe was of immense value. On the tomb were some carved ornaments, which I have copied, and some Kufic inscriptions, which I did not copy. Old festoons and Kashmir shawls were extended over and about the

[1] See note at the end of this volume.

place. Amongst the offerings was the very largest tiger-skin I ever saw; the tail was much shortened, but it measured altogether about twelve feet. The animal who wore it was killed by the Lohanis,—at least they told me so. I considered myself fortunate in not meeting with any serious misfortune whilst I was sketching. The better classes of passers-by were civil enough, in general; but the bigoted and inquisitive countrymen often looked very savage. One fellow wished to beat me, and another said he would shoot me if he had a gun; but the good old Kuzzelbash was ever at my elbow, and I never felt the least uneasiness. He always contrived to attract the attention of the bystanders from me to himself. At one time he would tell them I was only copying an inscription; at another, he would tell them seriously that I was a very great personage, come to take the command of the Ameer's army against the infidel

Sikhs, interlarding his stories with fifty anecdotes of other Feringis, whom he said he had known and attended upon. At Mahmud's tomb, where I expected to have met with decided interruption, I was astonished by his suddenly asking for a guitar (saringi), upon which he performed admirably. With this, and a little medical advice, and a couple of rupees judiciously given to the Fakir, their strong prejudices were so completely soothed, that I not only sketched the tomb as I could wish, but they themselves sat for their pictures with the greatest complacency, and gave me their "Khosh amdeh aid" (you 're welcome), when I had finished. "What are you doing?" I said to a Kashmirian servant; he was stooping at the corner of the tomb. "I'm only collecting some dust," was the reply; "Sultan Mahmud was a very great man." He would probably part with it for a consideration in Kashmir.

"Ghuzni," says Baber, "is a poor mean place; and I have always wondered how its princes, who possessed also Hindustan and Khorassan, could have chosen such a wretched country for the seat of their government, in preference to Khorassan. In the time of the Sultan (Mahmud) there were three or four mounds for collecting water. One of these, which was of great dimensions, was formed by the Sultan of Ghuzni on the river of Ghuzni, about three furlongs up the river, on the north-west of the town. The height of this mound may be about forty or fifty gez (eighty or a hundred feet); its length may be about three hundred gez (six hundred feet). The water is here collected and drawn off, according as it is wanted for cultivation. Allah-ud-Dyn Jehansoz Ghuri, "the burner of the world," when he subdued the country, broke down the mound, burned and destroyed many of the tombs of the royal family of the Sultan, ruined and burnt the city of Ghuzni, and plundered the inhabitants. In short, there was no act of desolation and destruction from which he refrained. In the year in which I conquered Hindustan (A. H. 932; A. D. 1525) I sent by Khwajeh Kilan a sum of money, for the purpose of repairing it; and I entertain hopes, that by the mercy of God this mound may once more be repaired," &c.—*Vide Leyden's and Erskine's Memoirs of Baber.*

After Mortazu Khan's advice I determined to proceed to Kabul by a way that he recommended, and because no other Feringi had ever been that way before. I should see the Bunde-i-Sultan, or Mahmud's dam, and a copper-mine; and I should find castles and villages the whole way; whereas, by the regular caravan-road, there was nothing whatever to be seen, and scarcely any habitation. My Hindustani servants, as usual, gave their opinion upon the great danger of being robbed at night; and their terrors were not decreased by their listening to the ever-frequent murderous tales of those who had never been by any but the usual way. My camel-man Kurrim was so determined on not going by any other than the usual road, that I was obliged to seize the head-rope of the foremost of the camels, and lead them myself till they were fairly moving in the way that I wished. My friend Kurrim had run off in a fright, under the apprehension that I was going to chastise him, but came back again before morning.

Soon after leaving Ghuzni I shot a churk falcon. It was, I believe, a young male; its length sixteen inches; breadth about three feet. It was a true falcon, having long wings and black eyes; the sides and top of the head of a dull reddish-white; back of the head dusky brown; beak green horn-colour; the breast and belly of a light, dull reddish-brown, with a single dusky spot near the end of each feather; the under-part of the wings was of the same colour, but lighter, and marked with narrow dusky bars. The whole of the upper part of the plumage was of dull brownish-grey; the feathers on the back slightly edged with brighter brown; the tail grey, with broad dusky bars near the end, and tipped with reddish-white; legs yellow; claws dark horn-colour. This bird is common in the plains of the Punjab, under the Himalaya, where it may be seen flying about the mimosas, from one single tree to another. It is a very swift and fierce bird. I have heard a kite scream as a churk was going to strike it, which it did apparently for hate alone, and passed on. I have no where seen it trained, excepting at Chumbah, a hill state on the north of the Punjab. It is flown at running game, and assaults the eyes; it is said to afford sport by attacking the porcupine. When in the air it circles very beautifully, whence its name "churk," or "the wheel."

The second day's march from Ghuzni I arrived at the Bunde-i-Sultan. The Emperor Mahmud had followed up the stream till he found it moving from an open space at the foot of the mountain, and through a narrow gorge; across the entrance he con structed a dam of rough stone-work, two hundred yards in length, and twenty-five feet above the sheet of water formed by it. Two flood-gates, one at the top of the dam and the other at the foot, regulate the flow of the stream, by which the entire of the valley to the westward of Ghuzni is irrigated. The whole is much out of repair. When I saw it the bed of the reservoir was half a mile in width, and nearly empty;

the stream forming a cascade of black muddy water, and rushing with great violence through the lower gate at the foot of the dam.

Some boys were groping for fish at the foot of it. I saw what I thought at first to be a small trout, which they had caught. It was, I believe, a fish similar to that taken in all the streams of the lower Himalaya. It was in splendid condition,—fat, and white as silver. I had now every reason to be glad that I had followed the old Kuzzelbash's advice. Our road lay usually through a narrow valley, that only wanted a few more trees to make it very pretty. Bearded wheat, barley, and clover, were growing near the stream; and a village and a fort were generally in sight; and on either side rose bare rocky mountains of granite, or limestone, from one to four thousand feet above the path. The natives were numerous, but peaceable. There did not seem to be a sword or matchlock in the whole country. The stations we pitched at were Killah-bin-Singh, Jugatu Killah, Ghurduni, Seiab, Lunga, Mydan (the Nawab's castle), and Kabul.

At Seiab, "the three rivers," I found Mr. Masson's servant employed in opening one of the numerous topes that are to be seen about the Kabul river, which we here crossed,—a clear rapid stream, containing, I believe, the fish already mentioned. They were emptying the well which is usually found in the centre of these buildings. I admired the man's honesty. I told him that I should shortly become acquainted with Mr. Masson, and that I was sure that gentleman would have no objection to my seeing the well opened. The man set himself down immediately on the top of the well, struck it with his trowel, and, with a good-natured look, affirmed that it was impossible. I subsequently saw the contents of this tope, with Mr. Masson, at Kabul. There are many such in the neighbourhood of that city. On the south of Kabul, on the mountains upon the right of the Peshawur-road, are two topes,—one, opened by Dr. Honinberger, proved to be the tomb of Kadphises, who, with Kanourkos, has given his name to a Mithraic dynasty, that probably drove out the Bactrians, and built the topes around Kabul. Several small vessels, bottle-shaped and cylindrical, composed of bronze, brass, and steatite, containing bits of bones and dust; little cylinders of pure gold, containing the same; rings, with or without jewels, usually a ruby; and gold pins, may be seen in the museum of the East-India House, having been found in these topes.

From this place I made a long day's

march up the stream, to see a copper-mine, at a place called Shibar. One is seldom repaid for going any distance to see a mine in these countries. The natives have a superstitious abhorrence of digging into the earth; the bold depths of our European mines would terrify them. In the present instance, after a fatiguing march, I found a hole in the side of the hill, not large enough for half-a-dozen persons to sit in. The hill itself was of slate, and the vein containing the ore was of quartz. Two men were working at it; and the produce of the mine, which is sold in the bazaar at Kabul, forms an item in the revenue of the Ameer. I robbed him of several specimens; and procured others of lajour, or lapis lazuli, which is also found in the neighbourhood. I was much refreshed by the hospitality of a friendly Khan, whose castle lay on the roadside. The fatigue would have been still greater had we not been regaled on some excellent bread and butter,—a luxury I had not tasted since I left Lodiana. The march over what is called the Mydan, or plain, is the only one where danger from robbers is apprehended; but we passed it without molestation. After a very long and hot day's journey we joined the usual caravan-route from Ghuzni to Kabul. The next day brought us to one of the Nawab's castles, Myrguzub, situated, with many others, on the plain called Chahar Deh, "the four villages," and only three miles from the city. These castles are easily described. They are generally quadrangular, with a tower at each angle. There is but one gate; the walls are of mud, but there are loose stones mixed up with them; and in the towers the floors and staircases are of wood. The Nawab's family were here. Four of his sons, very handsome boys, came running out to meet me, and commenced making inquiries after their brother Abdul Ghias Khan, who was educating at Lodiana in Captain Wade's school. As I was the Nawab's guest, with almost every European who has visited Kabul, I saw a good deal of his children. The eldest of the four sons, Abdul Ghuneh Khan, was a sharp, active, gentlemanly boy. I promised him a small telescope if he would learn the English alphabet. In three days he said it as well as I could, but would learn no more when my stock of presents was exhausted. They used to play at marbles after a fashion. Two of his little girls were sent to me, to have their pictures taken: one, who was a little tom-boy, would not remain quiet an instant; the other was frightened to death, burst into tears and afterwards sat still for half an hour. Tea and other refreshments were brought to me at the castle, and a messenger was immediately sent off to the city, to inform the Nawab of my arrival. He came in the evening, and entered my room

THE NAWAB JUBAR KHAN,
Brother of Dost Mohamed Khan of Cabul.

without giving me notice of his approach, and repeated his welcome, "Khosh amdeh aid," with warmth and sincerity, putting into my hands four or five old Mithraic coins as his offering. The Nawab Jubar Khan, who well deserves the name of the Feringi's friend, was then about fifty-five years old, to judge from his appearance; standing about five feet nine, with a corpulent person, dark áquiline features, and somewhat of a Jewish look, having a very good-tempered expression. His mother was a slave-girl in the Zunana of Poyndur Khan; his father gave her in marriage to a water-carrier, but still continued his attentions to her. By the custom of these countries, a servant marrying a slave becomes also a slave. When the Nawab was born, the waterman took the child to Poyndur Khan, and told him that he knew more about the child than he himself did. For many years the Nawab was running about the Bala-

Hissar of Kabul, and was called the waterman's son. Mahomed Azim Khan took notice of him, owned him as his brother, and procured him an appointment as governor of Dhera Ghazi Khan. He there became very popular; but still, like most governors in these countries, did not escape the charge of embezzlement. When Mahmud Shah, of Kabul, went to Sinde to collect revenue, the Nawab was called to account by the minister, Futteh Khan; who told him to produce three lacks of rupees, or that he would blind him. The Nawab prayed a respite; and, in the interim, presented Mahmud with a splendid scarlet tent; and, throwing himself at his feet, was forgiven, but deprived of the government of Dhera. He was soon after made governor of Kabul. His popularity rendered him an object of suspicion to Futteh Khan, and he fled to Mahomed Azim Khan, in Kashmir, whom he induced to rebel. The Vizir Futteh

Khan's forces were defeated in the valley; but he rode boldly up to Mahomed Azim's camp, and asked him how he could allow the Nawab to be the cause of a quarrel. Peace was made; but the Nawab remained in Kashmir till the Vizir was blinded. Upon that event, Mahomed Azim Khan marched from Kashmir towards Kabul, and left the Nawab behind him as governor. He was ejected, before a year had elapsed, by the victorious Sikhs. He subsequently received the government of the Ghilzyes, producing an annual revenue of ninety thousand rupees; but was deprived of it by Abib-Ullah, Mahomed Azim's son. Dost Mahomed Khan and the Nawab united, and drove Abib-Ullah out of Kabul. He then again acquired the government of the Ghilzyes; but Dost Mohamed Khan, the Ameer, had since taken it from him,—allowing him, when I was in Kabul, a revenue of seventy thousand rupees a-year, to which he added twenty or twenty-five thousand from his own lands; equivalent to about six thousand five hundred pounds a-year. His influence was very great; but Dost Mahomed Khan, his brother, is much his superior in point of ability, and seemed determined to be king, in spite of the disaffected, who were numerous, but disunited. He was supposed, however, to be a great intriguer, though he did not always pay attention to the treasonable messages and invitations that were sent to him. No Mussulman in power, in any country, can avoid intrigue, more or less. He is said to have communicated with Shah Shuja, in his hostile approach to Kandahar from Lodiana, in 1832. He then asked Dost Mahomed Khan to allow him to go and settle matters with the ex-king. The Ameer told him, it would be time enough to do that when his own forces were defeated. When the Nawab was governor of the Ghilzyes, he entered the hill country of

Taghau, was attacked, and lost his guns. Dost Mahomed Khan himself went the following year; and the Nawab wrote to the Taghau mountaineers, advising them to make a furious attack upon his brother, adding that he himself would contrive to withhold his assistance. He did this simply that his brother might not be able to laugh at him. The letters were intercepted, and coolly put into his hands by his brother, Dost Mahomed Khan; who, after he had taken the country, one evening, in the presence of his officers, kissed the muzzle of his guns, remarking that they were better than brothers to him. These are trifles in morals, when the characters of other Mahomedans are considered. Had he been brought up in contact with honest men, he would, I believe, have been as honest as any of them. His attachment to the English is the most singular part of his character. For the last sixteen years, I was informed that his whole wish and endeavour had been to induce the East-India Company to take Kabul under its protection; and though he had not met with much encouragement, yet there is no doubt but that the slightest advance on our part would have been eagerly listened to. His eldest son, Abdul Ghias Khan, has been for several years past at Lodiana, for the purpose of learning English; and I am much mistaken if he would not have sent one or two more, although his elder brother Dost Mahomed used to laugh at him, saying that the Indian Government did not treat his son with proper hospitality,—that is, according to their idea, did not pay the whole of his expenses.

The next day we were joined by Mr. Masson, the Company's correspondent at Kabul; to whom, as I have already stated, I am much indebted for information, alike instructive and amusing, regarding the hopes and fears of all parties in Kabul; and for much more which his persevering research—commenced and continued under unfavourable circumstances—amongst the topes, ruins, and antiquities, of the surrounding country, has enabled him to give to the world.

I was very happy to hear from the Nawab, in the truly oriental style of compliment, that all he had was mine, that the country itself was my own, and that I might do what I liked with it; that I might go where I pleased, sketch where I pleased, and make myself quite at home. He talked—mentioning their names—more or less, of every European whom he had previously known to visit Kabul, and to have been his guests; and he spoke of them all as his friends. He can neither read nor write; and, like most orientals, cared but little for the history of his country. I asked him who built the minars at Ghuzni. "How should I know," was his reply; and satisfied himself by further remarking,—as Mrs. Shandy did of the existence of Socrates,—that the building "took place a great many years ago!" Partly in order to show how anxious he was to please Mr. Masson and myself, as Englishmen, he drank off, in about half an hour, three as stiff tumblers of my English brandy and water as I ever remember to have seen finished in the same time. Although a Mussulman and unused to such potations, he did not appear the least affected by it. I presented him with a likeness of his son, Abdul Ghias Khan, then at Lodiana. Being afterwards curious to learn the fate of this drawing, I ascertained that it had been quarrelled for, and torn in half, in the Zunana; and that his younger brothers had then sold it to his old nurse for five rupees.

The Nawab and Mr. Masson preceded me into Kabul the next morning. By their advice, I had doffed my English shooting-jacket and broad-brimmed white hat, in favour of a handsome Multan silk turban and a native dress of English printed calico, which were presented to me, ready-made, by the Nawab.

WHITE MARBLE MOSQUE AT BABER'S TOMB, KABUL, LOOKING NORTH.

CHAPTER VI.

Character of the Country between Ghuzni and Kabul—A Kabul Dwelling-House—Aspect of the City—Bazaars—Climate—Description of the Bala Hissar—Variety of the Population—Origin of the Afghans—Neighbourhood of Kabul and Productions—Fruits, Flowers—Account of the Gardens—Manners of the People—A Bigoted Mussulman—Conduct of Dost Mahomed and his Sons to the Author—Sporting-Dogs of Mahomed Akber Khan.

THE character of the country through which I had travelled from Ghuzni, was that of flat and extended wastes, bounded by still more barren mountains. The dreary aspect of the scenery was varied only by occasional patches of verdure produced by irrigation from a village stream. But the Chahar Deh, through which I was now riding from the Nawab's castle to Kabul, was one mass of smiling vegetation. Shady orchards, and meadows, made verdant by artificial streams, directed so as to water them, were seen on each side of the road. Prosperous villages were on every hand, composed of square-topped mud-houses, surrounded by small patches of cultivated land, divided by rows of poplar, sunjit or willow. The crops appeared to have been produced by the united labours of the agriculturist and the market-gardener. I approached the city through clouds of dust, and took up my quarters in the Nawab's house. In order to arrive at the building, we passed up a narrow street near the bazaar, and stopped opposite to a place very much resembling the entrance to an English country inn stable-yard. This was the door of the Nawab's residence, and in the lane opposite to it, where there was scarcely room to turn a horse, lay a pool of standing water. The ladies of the Zunana, from whom I had so recently parted, were expected in a few days.

I was introduced into a court, or pateo, about eight yards square; on two sides were high blank mud-walls, and on the others were the apartments occupied by myself and servants. The windows, divided only by a supporting post of wood, were so constructed that they could be partially or wholly opened at pleasure, being merely carved shutters lifted by the hand, and made to rest upon a projection within a groove. The place of glass was supplied by carved trellis-work: the interior walls of the rooms were of plaster, with shallow gothic recesses, the ledges within which served the purpose of tables. The ceilings were of poplar stems, and long thin carpets covered the floor. The apartments were surmounted by a flat terrace of mud, around which ran a hanging fringe of trellis-work. The height of the walls prevented any one from seeing or being seen by persons in the neighbouring houses. I commenced exploring my domicile soon after I arrived—and contrived to get on the top of the wall, whence I had a fine view of the surrounding city, but I was observed by two or three men, who did not know I was the Nawab's guest, and who, jumping on the wall, commenced rating me for my impertinence, alleging that I could see into the Zunanas. They were soon pacified by a servant of the Nawab's, whom I called to speak to them. The description I have given of this house would be that, more or less, of all the better class of houses in Kabul. The Nawab's house itself—which I was afterwards allowed to see—was built precisely in the same manner, but much larger, handsomer, and cleaner. The doors, I observed, were generally so low, that a man—even of ordinary stature—could not enter them without stooping. This seems to be the case generally throughout the East. The houses are made so principally, I suspect, with a view to the advantage of resistance, in case of a forcible entry being attempted.

Let the reader conceive a broken succession of houses, composed of mud walls of different elevations, pierced here and there with wooden pipes to carry off the rain from the flat roofs, which it would otherwise injure; then let him imagine a few square low doors, opening under the eaves of the first story, projecting over a sort of trottoir, formed by the wearing away of the middle of a road, so irregular that no wheel-carriage could be driven along safely; now and then a larger door interposing,—the entrance to the residence of some great man,—with a mulberry-tree occasionally peering over the wall; add to this a thick crowd, and he will form a good idea of a Kabul street. The Bala Hissar or fort, the beautiful little white marble mosque near Baber's tomb, and the great bazaar, are the only buildings worth notice in Kabul. The profusion and display in the bazaar is perhaps nowhere else exceeded; though I do not think the bazaar equals some in Persia,—that of Shiraz, for instance. It must be borne in mind that the bazaar of the East is the arcade of the European city; excepting that in the former, mules, donkeys, horses, camels, and even elephants, are allowed to pass, as well as foot-passengers. There is room enough for all these in the principal bazaar; but in those of minor importance in Kabul, a countryman with a loaded donkey throws the whole place into confusion, thinking it very hard if the crowd does not give way to him. I well remember meeting a mule laden with grass, that was just entering a narrow street as I was coming out of it. I could only turn my horse with the greatest difficulty, and motioned to the driver to go back. He did so; but exclaimed aloud, "Is Dost Mahomed dead, that there is no justice?" This is a common phrase used by the inhabitants of Kabul upon similar occasions. It is hardly possible to ride through any part of Kabul without passing along a bazaar, consisting of a double line of stalls or shops, in which goods are exposed for sale, and in which artificers work openly at their different trades. The great bazaar has a vaulted roof; but over the inferior ones, during the summer months, branches

On Stone by J. B Pyne from a Drawing by the Author

VIEW OF KABUL FROM THE LEFT OF THE ROAD TO HINDUSTAN, LOOKING W.S.W.

London. Published by Whittaker & Co Ave Maria Lane.

of trees, covered with matting, are thrown across, for the purpose of obtaining shade.

The latitude of the city of Kabul is 34° 23′, nearly the same as that of Tripoli, Syria, Candia, Tunis, Madeira nearly, South Carolina, the centre of Japan, the south part of Corea, and the mouth of the River Hoangho. Its longitude is 69° 8′, the same, or nearly, as that of Hyderabad, in Sinde; the Chagos Archipelago, in the Indian Ocean; and Kerguelen's Land, more to the south, with Tobolsk and Nova Zembla, on the north.

The boiling point of water gave Kabul an elevation of about six thousand feet above the sea. From the middle of July to the middle of August, the thermometer stood at eighty degrees in my room. The climate is delightful, and cooler than Kashmir, and the sky remains unclouded for months together.

Kabul may be described as lying at the foot of a range of hills, whose direction is from north-west to south-east. The country is thus divided into the "plain of Kabul," and the "Chahar Deh," or four villages. The city is built directly under a rocky hill of gneiss, that rises a thousand feet above it, and bends round it from the south-east to the south-west; where, with the dip of another hill opposite, is formed the Pass which leads into Chahar Deh, one hundred and fifty yards broad. Through this pass part of the British army entered Kabul.

The Kabul river runs to the city, rising near Engeran, the castle of the Nawab Jubar Khan, so called, distant about thirty miles to the westward of Kabul.

After winding round the mountains which bound Chahar Deh to the north-west, it waters the plain itself, and reaches Kabul by the pass between the city and Asha Mahi (mother Eve). The water near the city is not recommended; and all who can afford it send for water to a small stream, which runs from the mountains of Pughman, and is converted to the purposes of husbandry. The whole of the north part of the plain of Kabul is irrigated by the water of the river; but the Logur or Mydan stream rises, I believe, near the copper-mine which I visited on my road from Ghuzni, passes from Mydan to Logur, and over the plain to the south of Chahar Deh; then waters the south-eastern part of the plain of Kabul, and is joined by the Kabul river below the gap in the mountains, close to, and to the north of, the Peshawur-road, a distance of fifteen miles from the city. The Bala Hissar, or upper part of the city, is watered by a cut from the Logur river, that comes from the narrowest part of the pass between Asha Mahi and the city. A strong wall, built by Khoja Saffir, is carried directly up the face of either hill; and is continued downwards, in the direction of the Bala Hissar, till its extremity is only divided from that fortress by a narrow road. The circumference of the Bala Hissar may be about a mile and a quarter; but not only the lower, but the upper fort—with its double and triple line of wall,—would, when I was there, have required not only repair, but considerable alteration, before an European engineer would have pronounced Kabul to be a place of strength.

The Bala Hissar was built by the Chaghutai or Mogul emperors. The walls are of stone, sun-burnt brick, and mud, thirty-five feet high. The residence of the "Ameer" is in the lower part, close to the parade-ground; but he had lately planned and laid out a new garden, called the Bagh-i-shah, with an open-fronted house at either end of it. Close to the Bala Hissar are the ruins of the Mosque called Musjid-i-shah; otherwise the Bala Hissar differs nothing in appearance from the rest of the town.

I agree with Lieutenant Burnes in estimating the population of Kabul at about sixty thousand. It is made up of Afghans, Kuzzelbashes, Tajiks, and Hazaras. Hindus are very few in number, and are chiefly money-lenders. There were about two hundred houses of Hindus at Bokhara. The Ameer of that place ordered the Hindus to bury, and not burn, their dead; which had the effect of making them leave the city. The Uzbeks of Koonduz call them, for some reason, their elder-brothers, and treat them with greater kindness than the other Mahomedans do.

Moollah Khoda Dad, a person learned in the history of his countrymen, read to me, from the Mujma-ul-Unsab (collection of genealogies), the following short account of their origin. They say, that the eldest of Jacob's sons was Judah, whose eldest son was Osruk, who was the father of Oknur, the father of Moalib, the father of Farlai, the father of Kys, the father of Talut, the father of Ermiah, the father of Afghana, whence the name of Afghans. He was cotemporary with Nebuchadnezzar, called himself Bin-i-Israel, and had forty sons, whose names there is no occasion to insert. His thirty-fourth descendant, in a direct line, after a period of two thousand years, was Kys. From Kys, who lived in the time of the prophet Mahomed, there have been sixty-six generations. Sulum, the eldest son of Afghana, who lived at Sham [Damascus], left that place, and came to Ghura Mishkon, a country near Herat;

and his descendants gradually extended themselves over the country now called Afghanistan. The meaning of the word Patan, which is synonimous with Afghan, has been already given from Lieutenant Burnes, signifying the "mast," or chief of his tribe.

The population of Kandahar is Afghan; in Kabul there are perhaps eighteen or twenty thousand Kuzzelbashes. Their history has been often written. When Nadir Shah marched towards Delhi, he had twelve twelve thousand fighting Kuzzelbashes with him. When he quitted that city, on his return, he left behind him three hundred of these, who, with other troops, were directed to bring away his treasure, and follow him. They passed through Kabul; but when, within two days' march of Kandahar, they heard of his death,—and, a few days afterwards, Achmed Shah, Nadir's lieutenant, arrived himself, attended by five or six hundred Duranis,—he seized the treasure, and took the Kuzzelbashes into his service; and his kind treatment of them induced others to come from the neighbourhood of Tabriz, Mushid, Kerman, and Shiraz, in Persia; where the true Kuzzelbashes exercise the profession of horse-breeders, shepherds, and cultivators. There are perhaps about ten thousand Kuzzelbashes in the city of Kabul, who are ever ready to draw their swords as mercenaries. Their leaders are by far the most wealthy, the most intelligent, and the most influential men at Kabul. The Tajiks are the aborigines of the country, and are not Afghans. Alexander probably found them there, as fire-worshippers, speaking Sanscrit or Pelhevi. The Hazaras, or Hazara Jat, are so called from the innumerable Taifa, or tribes, into which they are divided—Hazar signifying in Persian a thousand. They occupy the whole range of the Parapamisus, or the mountains extending between the Hindu Kosh, or Caucasus, and the city of Herat, to within a few days' march of Kandahar. In appearance, as I have already remarked, they very much resembled the Ghorkas; they have the same high cheek-bones, the same small eyes, very little beard, and no doubt are of Tartar origin. The Ghorkas, however, are Hindus; whilst the Hazaras are Shiah Mahomedans. This country is supposed to have been visited by the prophet Ali. There is a bunde, or water-dam, in the mountains near Ghuzni, said to have been miraculously placed there by him. There is also, in the same neighbourhood, a huge rock on the plain to the eastward, thrown by him, they say, from the top of the Sir-i-Koh mountains. In reality, Ali was never in these countries at all.

The Hazara mountaineers derive their

subsistence chiefly from their flocks. They prepare a coarse warm cloth from their wool, and find a ready sale in the plains for their cheese and ghee; the latter, it is well known, forming an indispensable requisite in the kitchen of every oriental, rich or poor. In their elevated valleys they cultivate wheat, barley, and rice. They have a species of wheat called, from its shape, dundan-i-shutur, or "camel's tooth." I regret very much that I did not know the existence of this grain until I had gone one march from Kabul on my return. It is nearly twice the size of the ordinary grain, if I were to judge of it by the few specimens that were put into my hand. The religious customs of the Hazaras are, of course, the same as those of Shiah Mahomedans. Their games are manly and athletic; they ride, wrestle, and shoot at a mark. I was several times informed, by different persons, that they will ride a race down the side of a hill at a speed alike fearless and astonishing. They throw a cowrie-shell on the ground, ride by it at full gallop, discharge their matchlocks at it, and usually strike it with the ball; and an apple is transfixed in the same way. The Hazaras have a yodeln, like the Swiss. I frequently heard it in passing through the country.

The immediate environs of Kabul have pretensions to as much beauty as most places that owe their improvement entirely to the hand of man. I am sure that there are not ten trees in the country that have not been planted; and I do not remember to have seen one that could be called a large tree of its species. The hills around are bare and rocky; the plain, by nature, is almost equally barren. A few wild flowers, such as tulips, are to be found; but time and human industry have been combining to create a soil from the detritus of the mountains, and to produce a fertility rarely exceeded. I have no where seen such an abundance of fruit. Of grapes, there are four or five different kinds; but I think that the husseini, a long grape, which is sent to India in cotton, in flat, circular boxes, is the only one that will bear competition with those of the south of Europe. The red melon is not better than our own; the white is sweet and delicious, but inferior, as I was told, to those of Bokhara, and I thought to some I had eaten in Little Tibet. The common apple much resembles the English red-streak; but they have a winter fruit which is far superior to it. The pear of Samarkand is excellent, very crisp and juicy, but still capable of great improvement. The European mulberry is called here the Shah tut, or king-mulberry, on account of its superiority to the insipid red and white fruit, so common all over the east. The peaches, apricots, plums, and cherries, are inferior to those of England. The pomegranates of Kandahar are the finest in the world, and their flavour is most delicious and refreshing. Currants, gooseberries, strawberries, oranges, and nectarines, are not known in the gardens of Kabul. Walnuts are plentiful. The Ruwash, or wild rhubarb root, I found to be too acid to be eaten without sugar; it makes a good preserve, and when well selected, forms an excellent ingredient in a curry. With a profusion of fruit on my breakfast-table every morning, I arrived at two very serious conclusions; one was, that I was sooner tired of any kind than of cherries; and the other was, that a fine mazagon mango was a finer fruit than a good peach. Potatoes that had been sent to Kabul by Captain Wade, from Lodiana, had been planted by the Nawab, and promised very well. In Persia they have long become common, having been introduced by Sir John Malcolm. Baron Hugel first introduced them into Kashmir, and sent them thence into Little Tibet. He forwarded since, if I am not mistaken, two hundred rupees' worth of potatoes, which were planted in the valley. The Kabul vegetables are excellent, but not numerous. They have cabbage, lettuce, turnips, carrots, onions, leeks, cucumbers, gourds, beans, peas, endive, celery, and cauliflowers. These are generally cultivated in the fields, the gardens being reserved for fruit and flowers. The system of irrigation prevails every where. The fields are divided by a ditch of running water; and on one side, perhaps on both, is a row of mulberries, willows, sunjits, or poplars. A patch of ground, contained in four sides of sixty short spaces each, is called a Jaryd; and in the same field is seen as many different crops as there are Jaryds, separated either by a water-course, or a small ridge of earth.

The gardens are surrounded by a mud wall; the fruit trees are all standards, and are generally planted without order, so that the garden has the appearance of an orchard. The walks are of raised earth, and between them are octangular parterres, loaded with common flowers, such as marigolds and stocks. These last are prized on account of their nocturnal fragrance, and are called the Shab-bu or night-scented.

The better class of the Afghans, and of all other eastern natives, pass much of their time in their gardens. They will remain for hours together, sitting on a carpet spread in the shade, talking scandal, or listening to the songs of their own musicians, who accompany themselves on the Saringi, or native guitar. Tea and the Kaliun are usually introduced, and often a substantial dinner. Wine is drunk now and then in secret, at private parties, but no female is ever allowed to be present. I was a guest at three or four of these déjeuners; at one given by Futi Mohamed Khan, the Nawab's father-in-law, I remember, that an old, bigotted, and good-natured Mussulman, was about to partake of some sherbet; but another by his side hinted that I had tasted it, upon which he put it down, and said, he did not like to drink out of the same bowl, with a man who had eaten pork. I could not help laughing at the man's grimace, and said, or rather made my Mirza say it for me, that I was very sorry to have spoiled his liquor, and would have been more careful, had I known he was so particular. The Nawab, whose guest I was, and by whose side I was sitting, seemed to think that the man had behaved rudely, and remarked that I had done perfectly right. And both he and the rest of the company, and Mohamed

Akber Khan, the second son of Dost Mahomed, who was present, joined heartily in the laugh against him. The young prince asked if I had eaten it often; I replied that I had, and it was in my opinion much better than mutton. No shudder, no expression of horror, followed my reply. So far was Mohamed Akber from being a bigot, that he has several times, when I wished to drink, ordered his servant to hand me water in his own cup. I think he would have been quite a European, had he resided a month at Lodiana. Knowing that I was a sportsman, he ordered his dogs to be brought, and asked me what I thought of them. I said that he must not be offended if I told him the truth: he replied, certainly not. I then said, that in England I would not have taken them as a gift: one being a half-bred Sinde hound, and the other a miserable cur of a spaniel. He was not the least angry, but, on the contrary, asked me to show him the worm-like fibre, under the tongue, which I said was found there; and I accordingly twisted up the tongue of one of his puppies, which he allowed me to bring on to the cloth off which we had just been eating. The puppy screamed with pain, and the prince with laughter, caring not a rush for the feelings of the other guests, who seemed horrified at the scene.

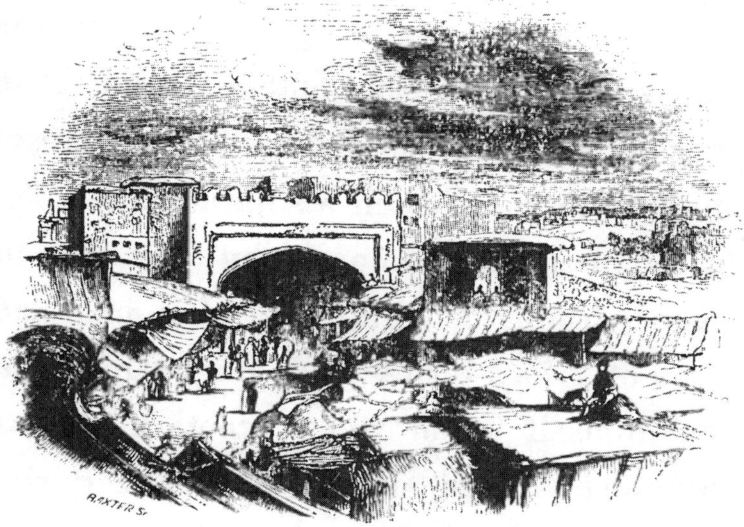

ENTRANCE TO THE PRINCIPAL BAZAAR AT KABUL, LOOKING E.S.E.—p. 160.

CHAPTER VII.

Durbar of Dost Mahomed—Allahdad Khan—Repast at the Reception—Give up Visiting Bamian—Professor Wilson's Remarks upon Bamian—Conjectures respecting the Route of Alexander the Great—Probability of the Macedonian March by the way of Bamian—Old Coins—Beghram—Baber's Tomb—Mosque of Shah Jehan.

WHEN the troops of Runjit Sing entered the countries to the west of the Attok, and approached the town of Tak, situated under the Sulimani range, and about one day's long march from Dhera Ismael Khan, the Rajah, Allahdad Khan, finding himself unable to resist such a superior force, fled through the mountains, by the way of Kanegorum, (celebrated for the manufacture of sword-blades and gun-barrels,) and put himself under the protection of Dost Mahomed Khan, at Kabul. The durbar was very fully attended, in order to receive him, in an open-fronted room, that looked over the new gardens, or Bagh-i-Shah. I made a point of attending: the Ameer and Nawab were seated side by side, and Allahdad Khan was introduced; he was a very slight, but handsome man, looking exceedingly unconcerned. The Ameer and Nawab rose as he approached them; they then embraced him, and made him sit down between them: he presented a golden-hilted tulwar, or sword, to Dost Mahomed, a couple of small guns, and an elephant, which was ridden up to the window, that the Ameer might see it. The Rajah's sons, and attendants, two or three of them in chain-mail, and all well armed, were then seated amongst the guests at intervals, according to their rank; one of them sat next to me, and talked much of the plundering mountaineers on their road. Trays of sweetmeats were then placed before us; and Allahdad Khan explained to the Ameer the movements of the Sikhs, from what side they had entered his country, all he had suffered, and how he had fled from the infidels. Upon which the chief Mullah in attendance, told him to be of good cheer, and to take courage, that God would protect his own, and not suffer the infidels to triumph. That, Inshallah Tállah! (please God), the Ameer would find him a home, and a new country, amongst the faithful, whose assistance he had sought. A repast, the best I saw at Kabul, followed; a ewer and basin of silver was presented to every guest, who received from it a little water in his right hand; white cloths were spread upon the ground, and upon these, before every five or six persons, were placed shallow wooden trays, containing the choicest specimens of Kabul cookery. A huge pilau of boiled rice, under which were buried shoulders and ribs of mutton, over-roasted, dry, and insipid, was heaped upon a large and valuable china saucer, which was placed in the centre of every tray. This pilau was not equal in appearance or taste to the pilau of Persia. Around it, in smaller saucers, were broken portions of mutton and chicken, roasted, boiled, or stewed up with eggs and spinach; a few preparations of milk and rice of different colours, some sweet, others acidulated; these mainly completed the dinner. The only dish that I had never seen before at a similar party, was composed of stewed quail. Afterwards, warm water was again handed to the guests, who sat with bared wrists, and their nails *en carte,* till their turn for ablution arrived. They finished by stroking down their beards, and growling out a Mussulman grace. They sat for sometime afterwards, with the utmost complacency, evincing the greatest satisfaction at the good dinner they had eaten.

With the countenance and protection of the Nawab, I was enabled to visit almost every place, that was worth seeing, in the neighbourhood of Kabul. One grand exception must be made. I tried hard to get to Bamian, but such good care did the Nawab take of me, that he told me he could only send me there with a large force, as the country was in a state of great disturbance, little short of rebellion, or disguised as a fakir. I therefore was obliged to give up, however reluctantly, the idea of seeing the idols and excavations of that celebrated place. When I first broached the subject to him, he stipulated, as a *sine quâ non*, that I should give the Naib Abdul Samud, a Persian general in the service of the Ameer, a bottle of brandy. I had refused it to him several times, because the man himself had asked for it in full durbar, and rather too familiarly for so short an acquaintance; but as he was known to be capable of any thing, as well as of instigating a robbery on the highway, the good Nawab thought it as well that he should be pacified. As the state of the country prevented my going, I may have some excuse for not hazarding much conjecture on the antiquities that are found there. Professor Wilson, however, has kindly favoured me with the following valuable remarks upon the subject:—

"If the traditions of the Persians may be "credited, we should look to Bamian as the "residence of King Lohrasp, the patron of "Zerdusht and the Magian religion; but, "as these traditions have been handed down "to us only through the romance of Fir-"dousi, it is not possible to say what cre-"dence they deserve. That a city was "here situated in ancient times, the posi-"tion of Bamian, on the high road from "India to Bactria,—lying as a valley at "right angles to the path, and between the "two passes of Kalu and Ak-robat,—ren-"ders extremely probable; but this proba-"bility is not confirmed by any facts derived "from the accounts of the expedition of "Alexander, who, there is every reason to "believe, must have followed this route on "his march to Bactria. He is said to have "crossed the mountains from Alexandria "'*ad Caucasum*,' to Adrasa, in fifteen days. "He must, therefore, have reached the

" table-land of Balkh in that time; and " there is no notice of his having passed " any city on his march. Bamian, then, " was not in existence, or it was founded " by Alexander. The pretensions of Be- " gram, however, to be Alexandria *ad Cau-* " *casum*, are much more tenable than those " of Bamian; and we must conclude, there- " fore, that it was not the site of a city until " subsequently to the Macedonian invasion.

" Although at this period there may " have been an extensive city on the site " of Bamian, yet it appears that the moun- " tains were not destitute of population; " and it seems likely, that at least in winter " time, the mountaineers sheltered them- " selves in excavations in the rocks, which " will account for the multitude of caves " found in this vicinity, and in other parts " on the same line. Thus the Macedonians " found, somewhere in the Parapamisan

" range, a cave, to which they attached the " fiction of Prometheus, and asserted that it " was in this spot that he was chained. This " is proof, therefore, of such excavations " being in existence, and of the purposes " to which they were applied. Even at a " later period, we have the evidence of " Chinese writers, who, speaking of the " people of Fan-yan-na,—*i. e.* Bamian,— " remark, that in the winter season the " inhabitants take refuge in caverns cut " out of the rocks *(vide Mélanges Asia-* " *tiques de Remusat)*. They are, in fact, " too numerous and too extensive to be " regarded as, exclusively, either catacombs, " or monastic cells, although they may " have been occasionally so employed.

" Of the sculptures at Bamian little " question need be entertained; they are " manifestly Buddhist, in the costume and " attitude in which Sakya is not unfre-

" quently represented when in an erect " position. The name of the place, Bhut-" Bamian, is possibly a corruption of Bud-" dho-Bamian; and in the designation of " the smaller image, Shah Muma, there " is most probably a popular version of " Shak or Sakya Muni; but whether this " etymology be allowable or not, the " figures are undoubtedly Buddhist. We " have every reason to expect Buddhist " images in this locality; for, at the end " of the fourth century of the Christian " era, Buddhism was the prevailing religion " of the mountain countries north of India. " One of the companions of Fa-khian, the " Chinese traveller, left him at Khoten to " cross the Hindu Kosh, to go to Ki-pin, or " Cophene *(vide Foe-Koue-Ki.* 22*);* which " must have adjoined, and probably com-" prised, Bamian; and, in the beginning of " the seventh century, the prince of Fan-" yan-na [Bamian] became connected by "policy and religion with China *(vide* "*Mélanges Asiatiques)*.

"Of the Buddhist character of all the "monuments at Bamian, Mr. Moorcroft, "who had been living amongst the Bud-"dhists of Tibet for two years previously, is "unexceptionable evidence. He says, vol. "ii. p. 391, 'my own conviction, from the "'character of the buildings, of the caves, "'paintings, and sculptures, is, that Bamian, "'whatever its ancient appellation, was the "'residence of a great Lama, bearing the "'same relation to the Lamaism of the "'West, as Lhassa does now to that of the "'East.'

"There is an apparent exception to the "general character of Buddhism in some of "the heads and figures painted on the rock "behind the necks of the images, for repre-"sentations of which we are indebted to

" Mr. Masson (*Journal of the Asiatic Society of Bengal*, vol. 188. 707. pl. xliv. p. 6). Of the three heads engraved, one has a crown like that worn by the Sassanian princes of Persia; and the same head, as well as a second, has a kind of ornament or wing rising from the shoulders, similar to a common accompaniment of busts on Sassanian sculptures and coins. There are also characters above the head of the larger figure which Mr. Masson has transcribed (*Ibid*, p. 188, and pl. vi. p. 241), and which he thinks resemble Pehlevi letters. Similar characters occur on a coin which he regards as Parthian, found at Begram (*Ibid*, pl. xliv). Mr. Masson would read the word 'nanaia;' but Mr. Prinsep justly objects to the reading, that this could not be applicable to the figure, as it is male, whilst 'nanaia' is the name of a goddess. He also observes, that the similitude of

" the marks, which Mr. Masson takes for " letters, to the Pehlevi alphabet, is but " just sufficient to hazard a conjecture upon " *(Ibid*, 188, *note)*. Whatever be the value " of these characters, we may admit, with " Mr. Masson, that the paintings are of the " Sassanian period, extending from A. D. " 220, to the era of Mohamedanism; but " it does not follow that the era of the " figures is the same. The political vicissi-" tudes of Bamian must have been the same " as those of Bactria and Kabul. We find " there the successive vestiges of Greek, " Scythian, and Sassanian rule, and of the " Buddhist and Mithraic forms of worship. " In the early ages of the Christian era, " and perhaps for a century or two before, " Buddhism flourished at Bamian; and such " of the caves as are appropriate to Budd-" hist mendicants were embellished, and " the statues of Sakya Muni were hewn out " of the rock. At a subsequent period the

" emblems of the worship of fire and fire-
" altars succeeded, until they were in turn
" displaced by the Arabs and the Koran.

" The etymological speculations of Wil-
" ford upon the name of Bamian, and the
" Parapamisan mountains in which it is
" situated, from 'para-vámi,' 'the excellent
" 'city of Vame,' are not entitled to much
" weight (*vide Asiatic Researches*, vi. 462).
" He furnishes no proof that such a city
" as 'Vame' is known to Hindus geogra-
" phers. The etymology proposed by Mr.
" Masson is scarcely less questionable; he
" derives Bamian from the Persian word
" 'bam,'—which, as it denotes 'roof,' may,
" he thinks, mean 'high land,' in opposition
" to 'daman,' skirt, or 'low land.' Para-
" pamisus he would derive from 'par' and
" 'pam,' signifying (he does not say in what
" language) 'hill' and 'flat.' That there
" may be some connexion between Parapa-

" misus and Pamir is possible; but he gives " no authority for explaining the latter to " signify 'the lord of hills.' Professor Las- " sen prefers the reading of Paropanisus, " and explains it to be the country upon " or along (pára) the Nishadha mountains; " the Nishadha mountains forming a range, " in the Pauranik geography of the Hindus, " north of the Himalaya.—*Vide Lassen* " *on the Kings of Bactria.*"

Professor Wilson proceeds to remark, that "the inhabitants of the country around " Kabul, at the earliest period at which we " have authentic accounts of them—that of " the Macedonian conquest,—were Indians; " and the designation given by the Greeks " is confirmed by the language upon the " reverses of the coins of the Greek kings " of Bactria, which, there is little doubt, is " a form of Prakrit, and is of the family of " those Indian dialects which are mainly

" derived from Sanscrit. During the reigns " of the Greek princes of Bactria, the go- " vernment of Kabul and the vicinity was " also Grecian; but the population must " have remained unchanged, as the foreign " masters—like the English in India at the " present day—were too few to exercise " any effect on the mass of the people. " The Indo-Scythians—the Yu-chi, or Getæ, " who succeeded the Greeks—entered the " country no doubt in greater numbers, and " may have been the ancestors of the modern " Afghans; at any rate, their government " was established at Kabul as late as the " fourth century of the Christian era,—as " is evidenced by the positive testimony " of Fa-Hian, the Chinese traveller. It is " rendered highly probable, by the quan- " tity of Sassanian coins found near Kabul, " that the Persian kings of that dynasty " held territorial possessions here subse- " quently to the Indo-Scythians, down to "the time of the Mahomedan invasion of "Afghanistan, in the end of the seventh "century; but it is also clear, from the "accounts given by the Mahomedan his-"torians, that the first invaders of Kabul "encountered Hindus, under native princes. "They soon, however, reduced the pro-"vince to subjection; and, by the end of "the tenth century, the Ghaznevide princes "had established their authority to the "right bank of the Indus. Since that pe-"riod, the country has been in the uninter-"rupted possession of the Afghans."

With the greatest possible deference to such an authority as that which furnished the preceding observations, I cannot but think, that the word Parapamisus is formed from the very commonly-used Hindustani word "pahar," which signifies a "hill" or "mountain," and which was perhaps the word meant by Mr. Masson; and the other word "pam," a "roof,"—that is, a flat roof, such as is used in the East. Mr. Masson informed me, that the Parapamisan range is a good deal broken into mountains, with table-land on their summits. Bamian, although in a valley, might have received its name as the capital city of the Pahar-i-Bam, or Pam; but this is mere conjecture. I would derive the word "pamir" from the same root.

The return of Alexander to a city he had founded amongst the Parapamisæ, is the best proof we have of his having originally crossed into Bactria, either by the pass of Bamian, or by that of the Hindu Kosh. As he came from the west, it is probable that he would choose that of Bamian, being the easiest, and the first he would meet with. But the learned Professor observes, "we may conclude, either that he did not go there, or did not find a city there." I

I should venture, with all deference, to think that Bamian, situated as it is and was, never could be without dwellings of some kind; and, although they might be so insignificant as not to attract the notice of Alexander, yet that the situation would not be overlooked by him. The first notice of *Alexandria ad Caucasum* is, that he went to the Caucasus, and built a city there. Ἐν τούτῳ δὲ Ἀλέξανδρος πρὸς τὸν Καύκασον τὸ ὄρος ἦγεν· ἵνα καὶ πόλιν ἔκτισε καὶ ὠνόμασεν Ἀλεξάνδρειαν.—*Arrian*, lib. iv. cap. xxiii. But this is qualified by the next, which says, that "from Bactria, the spring coming on, he pushed forward, with all his forces, for India; and, in ten days' space, passing over Mount Caucasus, he arrived at Alexandria, a city which he had caused to be built among the Parapamisæ, when he made his first expedition into Bactria." Ὑπερβαλὼν δὲ τὸν Καύκασον ἐν δέκα ἡμέραις, ἀφίκετο ἐς Ἀλεξάνδρειαν πόλιν, τὴν κτισθεῖσαν ἐν Παραπαμισάδαις, ὅτε τὸ πρῶτον ἐπὶ Βάκτρων ἐστέλλετο."—*Arrian*, lib. iv. cap. xxiii. Beghram is certainly not in the Parapamisus, which Bamian is; and if we are to pay attention to the hints of Eratosthenes, as related by Arrian, we should infer that the Macedonian soldiers, in their speeches, called the Parapamisus the Caucasus, by way of flattering Alexander. I am much inclined to think that the pretensions of Bamian to be the *Alexandria ad Caucasum* are far from being without foundation; and in that case, Alexander must have both gone and returned by way of Bamian; or, after having crossed over the Hindu Kosh, may have returned as far as Bamian, in order to visit his lately-founded city.

No one who has marched in the mountains, even with his own party, would, I should think, attach much importance to the fact of Alexander occupying sixteen days in his march from the city he founded, to Adrapsa, and ten only to return. Beghram is now a barren plain of many miles in extent, lying between the Kohistan of Kabul, and a small range of low hills opposite to it, those that bound the Koh Daman on the East. There are a few mounds upon it, and bits of brick, tiles, and old coins may be picked up every where. Mr. Masson told me that he attributed the number of coins, in a great measure, to the ancient custom of putting a piece of money under the tongue of a corpse. If Bamian be *Alexandria ad Caucasum*, then I would identify Beghram with Nicæa, or perhaps Kabul is Nicæa; both places lie in the route from Bamian on the high road to India, and in the Caucasus. Beghram is an open plain, and distant from the mountains, where the natives would hardly have ventured to oppose Alexander. Kabul is attainable through a defile, where he might have met with some opposition, and gained a victory, as the name would imply.

Kafilas will go with camels when they can; and all the year round goods are carried over the Bamian road, on the shoulders of the Hazara mountaineers. The Emperor Baber's tomb is close to the city, just within the plain of Chahar Deh[1]; it is surrounded by a large garden, the underwood of which is formed by bushes of the Alu-Balu, or wild cherry, which here, as well as in Kashmir, is planted for the sake of its white blossoms. Baber says, he caused the sour cherry tree to be brought to Kabul, and planted there. Over the tower grow a great many aspen trees, remarkable

[1] See Vignette, page 154.

from every part of the plain. Close to the tomb is a small, but very elegant, mosque of white marble, built by the Emperor Shah Jehan, in 1640, in honour of his great ancestor. It vies in beauty with any thing of equal size that I have seen at Delhi.

BUNDE-I-SULTAN.—p. 138.

CHAPTER VIII.

Afghan Horses—Fête—Tukt-i-Shah Mountain—Country around described—Mountains of Pughman—The Koh-Daman and Hindu-Kosh—Intriguers at the Tombs—Animal and Mineral Productions of the Hazara Jat—English Tomb at Kabul—Superstitions in Kabul—Genii—Visit to the Kohistan—Nawab's Barber—Timour Shah's and other Gardens—Relics of the Emperor Baber—Castellated Dwellings—Plain of the Kohistan—Vast Mountains—The Reg-Ruwan—Robbers—Religious Impostor—Return to Kabul.

UNDER the aspen trees, on account of the cool shade, are picketted the horses of the

Ameer, or at least a great many of them. They were noble animals, of the Afghan and Turkoman breed, usually sixteen hands high, and seemed much better calculated to go across a country, than those belonging to his formidable neighbour, Runjit Sing. Dost Mohamed had the advantage of the first choice, out of the caravans from Turkistan. I was present at a Fête Champetre, given by the Ameer in this garden, in honour of the arrival of Allahdad Khan, the Rajah of Tâk. The Ameer's sons, with the exception of Mahomed Afzul Khan, the eldest, who was absent during the whole time I was at Kabul, were there, as were also the Nawab, and all the principal grandees of the place. Carpets were spread in the shade, near the water. The day commenced with a dejeuner, and afterwards there was an exhibition of native dancing and singing, by male performers. They then contrived to while away the greater part of the afternoon in conversation, eating fruit, and saying their prayers. I amused myself with sketching a horse, belonging to the young prince Mahomed Akber Khan, who asked me to remain at Kabul, and draw all day long.

From the summit of the Tukt-i-Shah, which rises to the height of a thousand feet to the south of the city, is to be obtained the best general view of the whole country. It is noticed by Baber. The country around Kabul may be described as an extended plain, surrounded by bare mountains and hills of different elevation, broken into passes, up which the plain is extended. Across the great plain, as an axis from north to south, runs another chain of hills, of the same character as those around it. The Tukt-i-Shah is the highest part. On the west, at the foot of this hill, lies the plain of Chahar Deh, about ten or twelve miles in width, (from recollection,) and much longer. Its principal boundary is the mountains: on the south-east are the plains of Logur, and the open passes in the same direction. The Kabul river runs through the gap at the southern end of the ridge; and after traversing the plain, across which lies the road to Peshawur, is joined by the stream from Chahar Deh, which flows through the gap under the hill of Asha-mahi, and enters the mountains of Lughman, on its way to Attok. Kabul signifies, I believe, Cain. May it not be a corruption of τοῦ Καυκάσου πόλις? Mr. Masson would derive it from "Kapila," a city in which reigned a Prince Kanishka, according to M. Csoma de Koros (*vide Calcutta Asiatic Society's Journal, April,* 1834); and Professor Wilson tells me, that he thinks this etymology as probable as any other yet proposed. On the other side of the Hindu Kosh, they have the Dusht-i-Ham, or plain of Ham; and at Balkh is said to be the grave of Seesh, or Seth: Baber speaks of the plain of Lamech, the father of Nuh, or Noah, in Lamghan, or Lughman; and at Samarkand they show, so I was informed, a piece of Noah's ark.

To turn from the sacred to the profane, I may remark, that Charon, from his office, is supposed to be exceedingly rich; and an Afghan, without knowing much about the matter, in speaking of a wealthy man, will sometimes add, that he is "as rich as Kharun." They may have learned it originally from the Bactrians, who, no doubt, followed the ancient custom of placing a piece of money under the tongue of the corpse, with which he was to pay Charon.

On the north and north-west the horizon is bounded by the mountains of Pughman, the Koh-Damon, and the stupendous peaks of the Hindu Kosh, forty miles distant. Immediately below the Tukt-i-Shah is a spring, and a summer-house, much frequented by parties of pleasure. It is probably the Kelkeneh, or Gulguneh, of Baber. Many an intrigue is carried on by women, who leave the city, veiled, under pretence of mourning at the tombs, which are scattered over the foot of the Tukt-i-Shah. From the same place also, are dug up the old Hindu images, reliefs, and other relics, of which no account can be given, excepting that founded upon the reasonable conjecture, of their having been buried there, when the country first became subject to Islam. Dr. Gerard brought with him to Hindustan, a well-carved relief, which he had found at this spot. The lake which Baber mentions, to the southward of the town, was, when I saw it, but little more than a marsh. To the north, a few miles only from the city, is another small and very shallow lake, its waters brackish, and its margins whitened with a nitrous deposit.

In the mountains of the Hazara Jat, through which a footman will arrive in nine days at Herat, are black and brown bears, leopards, hyenas, wolves, foxes, and jackals. The ibex, the mar khur, and the mouflon, are common. I was informed, I do not vouch for the truth of the story, that at Korghan, about ten days' march from Kabul, and near the road to Bamian, there is a cave, from which a cold rush of air issues in the day-time, and at night a bright light, or flame, is visible. I was told that silver, copper, iron, lead, antimony, lapis lazuli, and asbestos, are found in different parts of the mountains around Kabul: the sand of the Kirman stream is washed for gold. The formation around

Kabul is of gneiss. On the top of a pass, on Asha Mahi, between the plain of Kabul, and that of Chahar Deh, I chipped off a small quantity of a green stone, that resembled the yeśhm, yu-stone, or jasper-agate of China. Exquisitely carved ornaments of this stone, such as sword or dagger handles, or mouth-pieces for the chebouk, or kaliun, may sometimes be purchased at a very cheap rate in Kabul. They are brought from Yarkund. The bazaars, too, are well supplied with many of the chemical articles, spices and medicines, which are used in Europe, such as sulphuric acid, the vitriols, corrosive sublimate, and mercury. The manna which is sold there, and is in great request as a medicine, is procured from Herat. At a burial-ground, opposite the Peshawur Gate of Kabul, is a tombstone, on which is cut in English letters, the name of — Hicks, the son of William and Elizabeth Hicks.

By its date, if I mistake not, he must have lived a hundred and fifty years ago. I could never learn any thing of his history. It may be inferred, that he was not alone when he died, unless we suppose him to have written out his own epitaph; but if so, his native place would have been mentioned. A field labourer earns about fourpence a day; a good carpenter or bricklayer can earn half a rupee. Rennell thinks that provisions in India are eight times as cheap as they are in England. In Kabul they are perhaps four times as cheap, with the exception of fruit; five seer—forty pounds English—of grapes, can be purchased for a rupee.

The existence of Gins, or Genii, is universally believed in Kabul, and, in fact, in all the Mohamedan countries. They can assume any shape, are of both sexes, and are of every religious persuasion, being

Hindus, Mussulmen, Sunis, or Shiahs. When a birth takes place in a Hazara family, food is put in a chamber, apart for the Gins, who will then protect and take care of the child, if it be handsome. In spring, they, as well as the fairies, disport themselves in orchards and flower gardens; and in winter, being sensible of cold, they are supposed to haunt old ruins and caves. If an ordinary person sees a Gin, he goes mad; but if he be a Syud, or descendant of the prophet, the Gin makes him a salaam, in an attitude of supplication, and is bound to obey the commands of the holy man. The Aals form another race of preternatural beings; they are said to resemble women of about twenty years of age, but with long teeth and nails, and with eyes that are curved down the side of their noses, and their heels placed where their toes ought to be. They are, I suppose, the Gouls of the Persian and Turkish tales, as they meet in grave-yards, and feed on the dead bodies of men and horses.

Several weak shocks of an earthquake took place whilst I was at Kabul. There are usually about a dozen in the course of the year. Baber describes a very severe one. The Mussulmen say that it is owing to the disturbance made by the soul of a great man passing from one place to another.

On the fifteenth of August, I started for the Kohistan of Kabul, accompanied by Mr. Masson, who said he would show me the plain of Beghram, whence so many Bactrian coins have, through his means, found their way into the cabinets of Europe. The word Kohistan, which signifies the mountain country, is more particularly applied to the large tract of flat country, which lies at the foot of the Hindu Kosh, or Caucasus, due north, and about thirty miles distant from Kabul. Koh-Damon, or the skirts of the mountain, is a name given to the open valley, which commences from the village of Shikardera, near the northern end of the Tukt-i-Shah range, and is continued thence with a varying width up to the Kohistan, being bounded on the west by the mountains of the Turkoman Hazaras, which branch off from those of Pughman, and join the Hindu Kosh to the northward.

Shikardera, "the place of the chase," where I had been previously, is about fifteen miles from Kabul. I rode there, accompanied, amongst other attendants, by the Nawab's barber, who is as important a personage as ever in an oriental establishment. I was received by his steward and his sons, at his own castle, and was lodged in a small room at the summit of a mud tower. The beauty of the situation, the salubrity of the air, and the fineness of the water, render it a very favourite resort of the dissipated great ones of Kabul, who drink wine, or bang, (a preparation from the outer bark of hemp,) in secret, and openly sing, smoke, and amuse themselves under the shade of the apricot trees. Timour Shah had a garden there, but it was in ruins. I walked into it, attended by a servant of the Nawab. An old man in charge of the building, was nearly getting angry with me, because I accidentally surprised his wife and daughters, who were busied over some fruit in front of the house. My attendant soon pacified him, and he showed us all over the place. The stone walls around reminded me of Little Tibet. In the neighbourhood were numerous vineyards, surrounded by them; but all was artificial; there was little natural verdure, and where cultivation ceased, the desert began. There are, perhaps, fifty villages scattered along the

Koh-Damon. Istalif (ustad or master, alif), with its large and beautiful gardens, lay in a nook on the mountains, several miles distant on the left of our road. Few quarters, says Baber, possess a district that can rival Istalif. A large river runs through it, and on either side of it are gardens green and beautiful. Its water is so cold, that there is no need of icing it; and it is particularly pure. The caravans that proceed from Kabul, across the Hindu Kosh to Khulum, pass through Charika, a long straggling village, near the foot of the Kosh. We slept at Bagh Aruk, a vineyard belonging to the Nawab, where the grapes had not yet ripened. The next morning we continued our ride northwards. There is no better description of Kabul and its environs, at the present day, than that of the Emperor Baber. The places he mentions are generally known by the same names; and I recommend the perusal of his memoirs to any who take an interest in Eastern affairs. From the road to the Kohistan we saw the Khoja-seh-Yeran, one of his favourite drinking spots, and mentioned by him: it is situated at a little distance up the mountain side; and the Bara-Deri, (twelve doors,) or summer-house, which he built, is still in existence; even the chenars which he planted are still flourishing. In a few hours, after a most picturesque ride, we reached the castle of our host, Beloch Khan, at Killah Bulund, or "the high fort." He was a tall and independent Tajik, who, having lately refused to pay tribute to Dost Mohamed, had just had half the wall of his strong hold blown down by cannon.

Every man's house is, in truth, his castle here; and innumerable are the quadrangular fortresses, scattered over the meadows, their neatly finished curtains and round towers rising with peculiar effect from the deep green of the groves and vineyards, with which they are surrounded. From the top of the bank behind the Killah Bulund, which has been formed by the stream of the Panjir, there is a prospect of excessive beauty: the plain of the Kohistan, ten or twelve miles in breadth, is plentifully and naturally irrigated by the divided waters of the Ghorbund and Panjir river, and thickly studded with turreted castles, vineyards, groves, orchards, and fruit gardens.

The plains of Lombardy, as seen from the Apennines, do not exceed the Kohistan of Kabul in richness or brilliancy of verdure, whilst the latter far surpasses them in point of situation, being backed by an amphitheatre of enormous mountains. To the left and north, are seen parts of the Hindu Kosh, below the limit of snow; and in those places where it was so steep that the snow could not lie, the rock appeared of a light gravel colour; while its peaks, towering far above the mountains in its front, appeared to rise to a height of seventeen or eighteen thousand feet. Below it, on the north-east, were the barren hills of Penjhir and Nijrau, both named from two fine distinctly-marked valleys, that lie at the foot of them. To the south-east, the Kohistan is extended to the hills of Taghau, and further away, to Lughman, the Lamghan of Baber, and so called, according to him, because the tomb of Lamech, the father of Nûh or Noah, is to be seen there. From Charika to Jelalabad the road is open, and I believe that Alexander, whether he recrossed the mountains at Bamian, or at Beghram, marched by this route towards India. It was, when I was there, too dangerous a road to be travelled in small parties. Two villages, named Bolergehin and Durnaneh, most romantically situated in different recesses in the mountains, are the principal nests of the marauders, who plunder the travellers of the plain, and afford a secure refuge for offenders from Kabul. Near them, at the foot of the mountain, was a tope, which was opened, not without risk of interruption, by Mr. Masson.

On a detached and comparatively low hill, a whitish streak is observed, extending from the summit to the foot of it. This is the Reg-Ruwan, or running sand, mentioned by Baber. The natives say that it runs up again, and that it is never diminished; and that there is a cave at its foot, where noises are heard, and into which the sand falls and disappears. It may be partly owing to the decomposition of granite or other rock, or to the peculiar shape or situation of the hill, which collects there the particles of sand taken up by the mountain gusts, or perhaps to both of these reasons, or neither. A drawing of the spot has, I observe, since been forwarded to Calcutta, by Sir Alexander Burnes.

Hyder Khan, the third son of Dost Mahomed, was at Charika, for the purpose of collecting revenue, and learning how to govern; but as we had no wish to expose ourselves to impertinent questions, such as how often we had eaten pork, or to a still more impertinent appropriation of any part of our property which he might fancy, we did not visit the place, but heard afterwards that he fully expected us. Some Hindus, who were reputed rich, and lived close to the plain of Beghram on our right, and who were in the habit of collecting coins, had absconded, *pro tempore*, from such a dangerous vicinity. So lawless are the inhabitants of this exquisite landscape, that our host himself said he dared not venture as far as the Reg-Ruwan; and that even if he found it necessary to send any one on a message towards the mountains, the man was obliged to divest himself of his clothes, for fear of being stripped and plundered.

As we were dining on the banks of the stream, a party of hill-men, who had been to Kabul to purchase matchlocks and powder, passed us on their return home. They all appeared frightened, and were hurrying on as fast as they could. One of them, a young savage, with a round red face and goggle eyes, had lagged behind, and came sneaking by us with two matchlocks on his shoulder, peeping round him in the greatest possible fright. It was very ludicrous to see him quicken his pace, when Beloch Khan roared out and asked him what business he had where he was. Mirza Gholam

Hyder, the Nawab's servant in attendance, who never said his prayers at Kabul for months together, when here thought it right to show that he was a good Mussulman, and knelt and bowed with the greatest devotion when the mullah of the place uttered the call to prayers.

We thought the outside of the castle would be cooler than the interior, and accordingly slept there. In the middle of the night we were awakened by a shot fired by one of our host's party, who was keeping watch. They immediately gave unsuccessful chase to a naked robber, whom they had observed prowling about our beds on all fours, and imitating the movements of a dog so well, that they were deceived by him for some time. This is a very common mode of approaching a tent in India.

The late chief of the valley of Nijrau was a more civilized being than his neighbours. He was a dabbler, after his own fashion, in chemistry, understood something of the difference and value of metallic ores, and would probably have protected any one who could have shown him any experiments, or added to his stock of information. But no strangers were, at this time, admitted into the country, excepting the venders of salt, and itinerant goldsmiths, who made up ornaments for their women of the gold which is presented to them by the mountaineers, whom they always contrive to cheat by mixing it with alloy.

Some years ago, a fanatic from the Kohistan took up his abode in a cave near, I believe, the Reg-Ruwan, and said that he was Imaum Mihedi, who is expected by the Mussulmen to appear at the end of the world. He collected upwards of twenty thousand men, many of whom dressed themselves as birds and beasts, and marched towards Kabul. They were met and defeated by the troops of the Vizier Futteh Khan. He then got some followers together a second time, and went through Taghau to Lughman, where he was again defeated by the late Sirdars of Kandahar, who happened to be then at Jelalabad. He returned to the village of Durnameh, where he died in obscurity.

I was prevented from having the option of visiting Mir Murad Beg, at Koonduz, by the non-arrival of a present, which I expected from Calcutta on purpose for him; and which, although it arrived in time at Lodiana, was not forwarded to me till two months after it should have been sent. Some presents of very inferior value, selected from my travelling stock, and forwarded with my letter to Murad Beg, were thought so unworthy of the occasion, that the minister who saw them refused to show either the presents or the letter to his master.

I procured a great number of coins at Kabul, chiefly Bactrian, or of the Kadphises group. I obtained a new gold coin, which was stolen, and one of silver, which was new, on which Professor Wilson will remark at some future opportunity.

A place called Rustum's well, into which he is said to have been thrown after his assassination, is about fourteen miles from Kabul. It is to be found near the southern end of the plain of Chahar Deh, in the direction of Logur. Mr. Masson received his information from a Gueber, or fire-worshipper, who had come from Persia on a pilgrimage to the place, and who spoke of its identity as being beyond a doubt. We contrived, however, not to find it, and returned to Kabul after a very fatiguing ride; and as I was to depart in a day or two, I did not make a second attempt.

GATE LEADING INTO THE FORT AND TOWN OF ATTOK, LOOKING WEST.

CHAPTER IX.

The Author quits Kabul—Different Routes—Sei Baba —Barik Ab—Jeg Delik—Arrival at Tatung—Jelalabad—The Sufyd Koh—Kaffiristan—Manners of the Kaffir People—Account of a Seor-posh Kaffir in Kabul —Dwellings of the Kaffir Race—Arrival at Peshawur —Reach Lahore—Khuruk Sing—No Nehal Sing— The Gurus or Priests—The Fakir Azij-ud-Dyn—Other Characters at the Court of Runjit—The Three Rajahs —Runjit Sing's Person—Introduction—Runjit's Notions of Physic—Military Display and Magnificence of Runjit.

On the twenty-first day of October, 1836, I quitted Kabul by the Peshawur-road, and slept at the Nawab's castle of Bukhak. About half-way we passed an old bridge over the Logur river, which forms a junction with the Kabul river near Bukhak; and thence, under the name of the Kabul river, passes through the defile by which it enters Lughman. There, so I was informed, its waters are precipitated over a ledge of rocks so as to form a cataract, which alone would effectually prevent a water-communication between Kabul and the Attok.

The road from Kabul to Bunu Tak is open, and not difficult, according to the information I have received. From Bukhak the traveller has the choice of three roads towards Peshawur; Khord Kabul, Sokta Chenar, and Lulah Bund; which meet at Sei Baba. I arrived there with my camels, by Sokta Chenar, in three days; the road generally good, but in places the rugged precipices meet so nearly that a gun-carriage could not pass. By the Khord Kabul road it occupies four days for camels. There guns cannot go, at least so I was informed. Horses can go by the Lulah Bund road, but not camels. Guns coming from Kabul to Peshawur arrive by Kohat. Sei Baba, a fakir's dwelling, is a regular nest of thieves; but the near presence of Mahomed Akber Khan, who was engaged in subjugating the valley of Taghau, which he effected after being twice defeated by the mountaineers, was a sufficient protection for me, and we passed unmolested. After his second defeat he had sent fifteen heads into Kabul. He had blown a robber-chief from a gun. "Why don't he rather march against the infidel Sikhs?" said a thief who came to look at us, but dared do nothing more.

We halted at a place called Barik Áb, a regular resting-place for travellers; there are caves hollowed in the bank for their accommodation. From the hills around there was a very extensive view of the country, in the direction of the Hindu Kosh, including the valley of Taghau, which appeared, from such a distance, to be nearly barren.

Jeg Delik was the next stage. A sort of police was established there, who resided in cottages amongst the hills, which were covered with holly-bushes.

The next day, October twenty-fifth, we passed a long red bridge, built by the Cheguthai, or Moguls, over the Surk Áb, a stream which emerges from a defile, and flows away to its junction with the Kabul river near the plains of Jelalabad. The whole formation here appeared to be of schist overlaid with sand and sand-stone. I slept at the village of Gundamuk, at the western end of the plain of Jelalabad; after refreshing myself with some very large grapes, brought from the Sufyd Koh.

The next day we arrived at the Nawab's castle at Tatung, near the foot of the mountain to the west of Jelalabad, where the steward had received orders to provide me with every thing. There is an excellent garden attached to it, in which the fruits and flowers of Afghanistan were mingled with those of India: the oranges and lemons of the Punjab were growing beside the pomegranates, grapes, and other European fruits of Kandahar. The situation of Jelalabad, which is a small plain, surrounded by a square wall, and containing five or six hundred houses, separated by a range of mountains on either side, preserved it generally from the chilling blasts of the western Caucasus, and the parching heat of India. A great quantity of sugar-cane is grown there. In the centre of the plain stands the town itself.

If Jelalabad be the Nysa of Arrian, as it most likely is, I should certainly think that the Sufyd Koh, or "white mountain," was Mount Meros. There is but little verdure on the other mountains around; and I have no doubt that ivy, perhaps laurel, and certainly rhododendron, might be found there. Ivy is plentiful about the old buildings in Kashmir, and, I believe, upon hills of the same elevation as the valley. The majestic and isolated appearance of the Sufyd Koh, independently of its skirts being partially covered with jungle, would undoubtedly, I should think, attract to itself attention, as a locale on which a tradition might be founded.

The Sufyd Koh, or "white mountain," forms a most majestic boundary to the southern side of the plain, at a distance of about fifteen or twenty miles from the town. Its height, at a guess, is about seventeen thousand feet; and, along the whole southern side of the Himalaya, from the Hindu Kosh to Nipal, the Sufyd Koh is, I believe, the only detached mountain which can vie in altitude with the more connected peaks of that stupendous Cordillera. I regret that a want of time prevented me from visiting it. The productions of this mountain are said to be numerous. I can answer for the goodness of its pomegranates, which are of the same kind as those of Kandahar; and for the large size, rather than the flavour, of its Kuttah grapes. Most of the fruits of Kabul are cultivated on its rugged declivities; and all the wild animals that haunt the neighbouring mountains, near and distant, are numerous in its recesses. The tiger is said to be well known there.

The snowy top of the Sufyd Koh is visible from Peshawur; but it cannot be seen from Kabul, even from the top of the Tukt-i-Shah, which rises behind it.

I regretted still more that I could not go to a village situated on the borders of Kaffiristan, a long day's march from Jelalabad, where savage-looking mountains elevate themselves to the north. The good Nawab had made arrangements for me to go there, if I wished. I forget its name; but it is well known, as being inhabited both by Mussulmen and Kaffirs, who act as the sentinels or out-pickets of two opposing armies, to prevent invasion from either party. No persons but the venders of salt and itinerant workers of golden ornaments are allowed by the Kaffirs to enter their country.

Kaffiristan commences from the mountains beyond the valley of Nijrau, to the north of Kabul, and extends behind those of Taghau and Lughman to the frontiers of Bajawur. To the north it is bounded by Badukshan; and it forms the greater part of one side of the valley of Chitral, or Little Kashghar. The Kaffirs are on good terms with the Chitralis, and occasionally mix with them. My authority is the grandson of the exiled Rajah of Chitral, who was driven out by the present ruler, Shah Katore. I saw him in Little Tibet. The Mussulmen regard the Kaffirs, according to the name they give them, as infidels; the Kaffirs, on the other hand, detest the Mussulmen. The feuds between them are constant, and there are persons killed every year in Lughman. Such is the animosity that exists towards the Mussulmen there, that when a return from a foray is expected, the young Kaffir girls put walnuts and dried fruits into their bosoms, and advance to meet the men returning, who flourish their long knives, with the heads of their victims upon the points. Those who have killed a Mussulman have then a right to snatch the walnuts and fruits from the girls' bosoms. When a cow is to be eaten at a feast, those who have not been blooded by the death of a Mussulman have their food handed to them over the carver's shoulder, and are pelted with cow-dung by the women. This almost unknown race say that they are Arabs, and are descended from the same tribe as Mahomed. I should think it much more likely that they are descended from the Greeks of the Bactrian dynasty. I saw three Kaffir slaves; one of them at Kabul, and another at Jelalabad. They had grey eyes, light brown hair, and a complexion that would have been considered fair in Europe; and their manner was very different from that of either Sikh, Hindu, or Afghan. One I saw at Kabul was a young man, about eighteen, who said he was the son of a Malek or chief among his countrymen. He and his brother were crossing the country to visit another brother, and fell in with a party of Mussulmen, who made him a prisoner. His features were highly intellectual; he was an admirable shot with a bow and arrow. There was a natural freedom and elegance in his manners; and in that of a second particularly, who was the youngest, and whose action, when he wished to speak, but was unable to express himself, was worthy the study of a sculptor. They were learning to read and write Persian; and their abilities were said to be extraordinary. The youngest of all, a little boy, was caught by the Mussulmen whilst tending sheep; and, at the command of his master, he showed me how his captors suddenly put one hand over his mouth, and the other over his eyes, when he was made a prisoner. He afterwards stretched himself out on the ground, to show me how he was measured and sold according to his height, which was five spans, at twenty rupees a span. With the assistance of the eldest of these Kaffirs I was able to form a vocabulary, which appears in the appendix, and bears but little resemblance to Greek.

The houses in which the Kaffirs dwell are some of them three or four stories high. From what I could collect, many of their occupants were accounted rich amongst them; and not without reason. Their flocks and herds are very large; and the golden ornaments of the women are far from valueless. I was told that they rarely inhabit the valleys, but that all their dwellings were placed on the mountain side, with a regard to the vantage-ground in case of attack, and a distant view of foreign invasion. The poorest of them drink wine, made in the country; and their fondness for the liquor is shared by many of the inhabitants of the valleys on the north-east of them. The Gilghitees, for instance, drink wine in abundance. I have tasted it; it was not bad, but required clarifying. Whilst their drinking-vessels would assimilate them to the Greeks, their exposure of the dead rather bespeaks for them a descent from the Guebers of Persia; and they themselves say that their forefathers were Arabs.

I have no remark to make upon the numerous places which, according to Arrian, Alexander met with and took in his march from Nicæa to the Attok; excepting, that as elephants and a large breed of cattle are mentioned, they must certainly, with the exception of Aornos, have been in the plains.

Dost Mahomed Khan and his brother the Nawab had furnished me with a paper to Saadut Khan, the chief of the Mohmunds;

and I passed the insolent scrutiny of that lawless and largest tribe of Afghans with safety, and a reasonable amount of black mail. Saadut Khan sent me word that he waived his share, but that the tribe must have theirs, and would take no denial.

I arrived at Peshawur on the third of November, 1836. Saadut Khan's servant attended me over the Kabul river, and did not return till he said that he dared go no further on account of the Sikhs.

I called upon Shere Sing, the eldest adopted son of Runjit, who was encamped near the place, and presented him with a handsome telescope, which I had intended for Murad Beg of Kunduz, and which only arrived as I was entering Peshawur. I got in return, by way of compliment, a guard of twelve horsemen as far as Attok. I have twice seen Attok: the first time the river at the bridge was only eighty yards in width, and at this time it was about one hundred and twenty; but the current was deep and rapid, and looked as if it would sweep away any obstacle.

I had obtained from Runjit, through the intercession of General Ventura, a permission to visit Kashmir a second time. I had never seen any of the country to the north of the Jalum. In my way thither I visited Torbela, where the Maharajah Runjit Sing once forded the river on an elephant, having first propitiated the river-gods, so I was informed, by turning a live elephant into the stream to take his chance. My Sikh informants would have me believe that there was no ford previously; but that the Maharajah, being a Khoda-Dad, or "God-given," he alone was enabled to find the ford. The river there is tranquil, but rapid, about two hundred yards in width. The Sikhs had a small fort there. I thence pushed on to Kashmir, *via* Mazuferabad and the Baramula pass; and afterwards arrived at Lahore, and remained there in order to be present at Sir Henry Fane's visit to Runjit, in March, 1837.

The great grandfather of the late Maharajah, "maha" signifies "great," was a Zemindar or land-owner, whose chief wealth was, however, derived from the valuable produce of three good wells. But I have no intention of detailing the history of his family; and those who wish to be made acquainted with its rise to power, and to read a general notice of the Sikhs, should consult Sir John Malcolm's work, Mr. Prinsep's life of Runjit Sing, and Mr. Osborne's recent publication.

At the period I am speaking of—and, in fact, up to the day of Runjit's death—the first in rank at the court of Lahore was, of course, the Kunwur or "Prince," Khuruk Sing, who succeeded his father, but has been since deposed. He certainly resembled him in feature, but in no other particular; having nothing of that superior intellect of which Runjit had made so good a use. His only son, No Nehal Sing, ("the new stem or tree of the Sikhs,") was a great favourite with his grandfather,—an incipient Hotspur, of whom great things were expected; even that he would again sway the sceptre of the Moguls on the throne of Delhi. Such, however, was Runjit's jealousy, that both Khuruk Sing and No Nehal Sing were closely watched, and rendered comparatively powerless with regard to any influence arising from property, or the number of their adherents.

The adopted sons of Runjit were the next in rank. They were usually named after his conquered provinces, Multan Sing, Kashmir Sing, &c. Shere Sing, the eldest, was a great favourite with the army. Shere Sing was allowed to sit on a chair by the side of the Maharajah; or in front of him, if the heir-apparent and his grandson No Nehal Sing sat by his side. His young favourite, Rajah Hera Sing, "the diamond lion," son of the minister Rajah Dhihan Sing, was, however, usually allowed to occupy a place beside him. Shere Sing means, literally, "the lion-lion." The word "Sikh" signifies a "disciple" or "learner," from the Hindustani word "sikhna," "to learn." They profess to learn every thing from their great Gurus, or priests, who composed the Guruntb, or holy book of the Sikhs. "Sing," or "Singh," is a "lion," and is a title which is assumed by almost every Sikh, whether he be a Sepahi or not.

The Gurus, or priests, were also allowed

to sit on chairs in the Durbar. The Gurunth, being the sacred book of the .Sikhs, is allowed a guard of honour; and, when talking to a Guru, it is the etiquette to inquire after the health of the Gurunth Sahib; which would be paralleled, in English, by an inquiry after the health of — Bible, Esq. When Runjit was encamped away from his capital, and the Gurunth was expected to arrive on a subsequent day, he would ride out to meet it, and dismount, and salaam to it, with the greatest reverence,—so I was informed; but I never had the good fortune to witness the incident. Runjit, however, was never remarkable for a very conscientious or practical observance of any of those great truths upon which all real religion must be based. He knew, as all great rulers have known, the advantage of a national religion, and a show of respect for its ordinances; but I much doubt if he cared for it at heart; whilst the quantum of superstition was, as is usually the case, inversely to that of the real religion he possessed.

The cow is venerated by the Sikhs, even more than by the Hindus. The former were besieging a fort on the Indus, and heard that the Patan garrison had killed a cow; when they took it, they put every one to death. An unfortunate Mussulman, at Peshawur, was found guilty of eating roast beef; the Sikhs kindled a large fire, placed their victim within the circle they formed around it, prevented his escape by thrusting pointed sticks at him, and so burnt him alive.

The Fakirs, Aziz-ud-Dyn, "the delight of the faith," Nur-ud-Dyn, "the light of the faith," and the youngest brother, whose name I forget, were originally barbers. A Fakir is not necessarily a mendicant, according to our European idea of the term. The word "Mirza," in Persian, prefixed to a name, would denote his office as a "teacher," or "secretary;" but it becomes merely a surname when another is prefixed to it, as is the case with the royal family of Persia, who are called Abbas Mirza, Suliman Mirza, &c.

The Fakir Aziz-ud-Dyn was the chief secretary and confidant of the Maharajah; and was usually employed in company with Lallah, "teacher," or "professor," Govind Jus, whose brother, Kissen Chund, was the Vakil, or Sikh political resident at Lodiana, in conducting a discussion with the Honourable Company's political agents. The Fakir Nur-ud-Dyn was deputed to wait upon visitors or Europeans wishing to enter his master's service. The youngest was entrusted with the care of the treasure in the fortress of Govind Ghur, near the city of Amrit Sir, or Sar,—"the ambrosial lake." The three brothers usually corresponded in a cipher, which was known only to themselves. They displayed great shrewdness and cunning in the transaction of business for their master; but there was always a mild urbanity, and much of real kindness, in their manner and conversation. The Jemadar Kosheal Sing; the Sirdar Hurri Sing, who was killed in an action with the Afghans in the Khyber pass; Futi Sing, the chief of Kopatella; Lena Sing, and his brother Guja Sing, with many others, were possessed of great wealth and influence in the Durbar.

To the French and Italian officers in his service Runjit Sing is mainly indebted for the formation of his disciplined troops, and, no doubt, for much good and general advice; but their services have never received an adequate requital; and so jealous was he of an increase of their influence in his country, that he had never allowed either of them even to visit Kashmir; but being, at the same time, fully aware of their importance to him, he used to secure their residence in his country by keeping their pay constantly in arrear. When I quitted the Punjab, Runjit was also availing himself of the able, but ill-requited, services of the following officers: Captains Ford, Foulkes, Steinbach, De la Font, De la Roche, and Van Cortlandt.

The most powerful of the Sirdars were the three brothers, Rajah Gulab Sing, of Jumu; Rajah Dhihan Sing, of Bhimbur; and Rajah Sucheyt Sing, of Ramnagur: three towns in the lower range of the Punjabi Himalaya. Rajah Dhihan Sing, the prime minister, was originally little more than a common suwar, or mounted Sepahi; with a pay not exceeding seven rupees a-month. His handsome appearance—his skill in martial exercises—and his address in the hunting-field, procured him the especial favour of Runjit; who eventually created him the Rajah Rajghan, or Rajah of Rajahs; and he was always called, *par excellence*, "Rajah Sahib," or "the Rajah." Up to the time of his master's death he was his prime minister of the Punjab. He filled his office with ability and distinction; and, perhaps, notwithstanding his faults, and a studied, but dignified, insolence of demeanour, he was one of the best men, and the finest fellow, in the Punjab; which is not, however, saying much for him. He really was attached to Runjit; but his pretended attempt to throw himself upon his funeral pyre, was nothing but a masterly piece of humbug. When his influence was sufficiently established he introduced his elder brother, the present Rajah Gulab Sing, to Runjit. He, also, was only one of the better class of mounted Sepahis. His career has been much stained by treachery and perfidy. He is now Rajah of Jumu, at the foot of the mountains; and the most powerful man in the Punjab. He occasionally commits acts of the greatest ferocity; such as skinning his prisoners alive. Rajah Sucheyt Sing, the youngest of the three, is a cipher, when compared with either of the others. He likes the English far better than his brothers do; and they do not, it is said, like him the better for that. He is effeminately handsome, and is always splendidly dressed. These three brothers have long been masters of the Alpine Punjab, with the exception of the valley of Kashmir; for the seizure of which they have been long preparing. Rajah Gulab Sing, having taken Ladak, the capital of Middle Tibet, in 1835, has since been intent on the occupation of Little Tibet; for the purpose of completing a military circle around Kashmir, and of being able to pour his troops into the valley from every side, immediately upon the death of Runjit. Captain Wade,. as political agent at Lodiana, was unable to assist Ahmed Shah, of Little Tibet, as he could wish; being prevented from doing so by the terms of the ill-advised treaty of Rupur, of which more afterwards; by which Runjit was allowed the benefit of the Company's non-interference with any expedition which he or his officers might undertake on the west side of the Sutlij. His hints and intercessions on behalf of Ahmed Shah were, however, attended with a beneficial effect; and my own presence in Little Tibet, aided by that of Dr. Falconer, in 1838, with no other merit but that of being an Englishman, and the first European that had ever set foot in the country, has, since my first visit to it in 1835, been mainly instrumental in deterring Gulab Sing from invasion, for fear of giving offence by making war upon a state whose Chief was affording a right hospitable reception to a British traveller.

The wealth of the three Rajahs was said to equal that of Runjit; and their power was such, that latterly Runjit himself was afraid of them. They reigned over the mountain territories of about five-and-twenty Rajahs, who have either been deposed or degraded by them, or through their instrumentality; and I think that the best line of policy that the Indian Government (whom, by the way, they cordially hate) can adopt, when it has the opportunity, is to follow up that display of its love of legitimacy which it has so lately evinced at Kabul, by reinstating the rightful Rajahs upon their Ghuddis. To say nothing of the propriety of dividing the power of the Chiefs, it would be also the surest way of gaining the affections of their people. In several instances I have been asked, indirectly, rather than openly, for my intercession with the British Government; and it was every where evident, that nothing but the presence of Rajah Gulab Sing's people, who were always with me, prevented a similar application at every place I came to. Gulab Sing, in particular, is hated and feared for his tyranny; and all three are despised by the lovers of legitimacy, because they are not Rajpoots, but are only Dogras, ("do," two; and "rug," a vein,) of mixed blood and low caste. The abilities of the two elder brothers are certainly of a high order; but it is not on that account that they find themselves where they are, for the possession of them would otherwise have operated to their detriment. Their power would never have been allowed by Runjit to increase as it has done, had it not been for his fondness for Hera Sing, Dhihan Sing's son. During the latter years of the Maharajah's life it amounted to an infatuation; and this spoiled child and enfant chéri de la fortune was refused nothing by his Sovereign, and played his cards so well, that he made his own fortune, and protected that of his father and uncles. He was, probably, when Runjit died, one of the richest men in the Punjab. But I shall have further occasion to notice these subjects when treating of Kashmir.

The diminutive size of his person, and the comparative simplicity of his attire,—consisting of a turban, usually large only over the forehead, with the end hanging down the back, folded à la Sikh; a kind of frock or tunic, padded so as to give an extraordinary breadth to his naturally wide shoulders; the kumerbund tied round his waist; and a pair of close-fitting trowsers, of the same colour, yellow, or pea-green; and all of Kashmirian manufacture,—did not prevent any one, who entered the Durbar for the first time, from instantly recognizing the Maharajah. The contour of his face was square; his complexion was a light olive; his forehead was wide and Napoleon-like; his right and only eye, large and prominent, for he had lost the other by the small-pox, with which he was slightly marked, was incessantly roving; his nose was slightly *retroussé;* his nostrils expanded and contracted, as his conversation became animated; and decision and energy were pre-eminently imprinted on his thick but well-formed lips. A grey mustache, blending with his white beard, added character to the very expressive countenance of this extraordinary man.

It was on my return from Kashmir and Little Tibet, in 1835, that I was first introduced to the Lion of the Punjab. From

Kashmir to Lahore I had enjoyed the agreeable society of Baron Hugel, to whom, as an Ali-Dja, or nobleman, Runjit had paid every distinction, during the whole time he had remained in his country. A display of fireworks greeted his arrival at Anar-Kulee, or "the blossom of the pomegranate," the residence of General Ventura; and the drawing-rooms of our kind host, of which the ceilings and wainscots were entirely covered with paintings, and glass mirrors in gilt frames, à l'orient, were no unsuitable theatre for the performance of Runjit's dancing girls, of whom the choicest were in attendance every evening.

Runjit soon sent for us; and we repaired to his presence, in company with the two fakirs, Aziz-ud-Dyn and Nur-ud-Dyn. We were also accompanied by Lieutenant Mackeson, the assistant Sikh political agent, who had come to Lahore upon some public business, and was residing at General Ventura's. He acted as interpreter for us. We found the Maharajah seated in a small room in the palace; one which he usually occupied, because he could thence see his guard, and his favourite horses, which were picketed close by. We both bowed; and, according to custom, passed a bag of rupees around his head, to keep off, as it is said, the evil eye, or evil spirits, and then presented it to him. He shook hands with us, requested us to sit down, and immediately commenced a conversation with Baron Hugel. Hera Sing was seated in a gilt chair on his right, and a few more of the Sirdars were either sitting or standing around us. His questions were short and comprehensive, and related chiefly to military subjects, —what service the Baron had seen, whether he thought cavalry or infantry the strongest arm, adding that his French officers told him that their squares would beat off all his cavalry,—whether he was related to the royal family of Austria. He then turned to me, asked me a few questions about my travels, and whether I knew any thing of military discipline; and, as I answered him at once in the negative, he seemed careless about further inquiry, and we soon took leave of him. The next morning the fakir was again sent to put questions to the Baron,—"How would he act if he had but a handful of troops to oppose to a more numerous force?" to which he answered, "that it would be necessary to concentrate them, and be more active and vigilant in proportion to his inferiority." The fakir smiled at this, as he knew it would please his master. "And which of the European armies do you think the best disciplined?" "The English," was the flattering reply; and the old minister smiled again, with still greater satisfaction, and then summed up his queries with what both he and his master no doubt considered to be the very climax of compliment,—which was a request from Runjit, that the Baron would give him a little of the very same medicine which he took himself. As there was no help for it, I went out of the room, and returned with my bottle of calomel, and handed it to the fakir, with many remarks on its strength, cautionary, but useless, as there was not the smallest chance of Runjit's touching a single grain of it.

Every morning brought with it some new display, and an invitation from Runjit. His Sepahis, in chain armour, were exhibited; his picked matchlock-men fired at a brass tota, or waterpot, and worse shots I never saw. He then requested the Baron to point a gun at a tree, as a mark ; and was pleased to see it shivered by the third shot.

At one of these interviews Runjit took

my hand at parting, and asked me "if I thought I could manage a country?" I said, "that I believed I could;" but, knowing what was coming, I could not help smiling. He smiled also; but added, "and do you think that you could restore a dilapidated country to its former prosperity?" At this I fairly laughed in his face; at which he looked serious, and was, or pretended to be, offended; and, at the next meeting, he hardly returned my bow. The fact is, that he tried to humbug almost every European he saw into the idea that he would make him governor of Kashmir; whereas, in truth, he would as soon have had the devil for his viceroy in that fine province, and was far too apprehensive of a strike for independence, to entrust its government to an Englishman. Strange to say, Runjit had never visited Kashmir, though he has had possession of it for the last twenty years. He has been deterred, perhaps, by three reasons: the fear of a rise in the Punjab during his absence; an unwillingness to put himself in the power of the hill Rajahs; and the idea that the air would be too cold for him; and, very possibly, from some superstitious motive besides.

It was on a glorious afternoon of one of the finest days of an Indian winter that we were summoned to attend Runjit, in order to witness a review of his regular troops. The sky was cloudless; the sun most brilliant, but not oppressive. The hedgeless parade-ground of Lahore, with its white summer-houses, and its gardens and groves of palm, mango, and mimosa, looked clean and verdant as an emerald. On the south it was bounded by the lofty walls of the Imperial city, and the palace roofs, musjids, domes, and minars, that rose majestically above it. The plains of the Punjab, endless to the westward, were apparently extended on the north and east, without any inequality of surface, to the very foot of the Himalaya, of Kashmir, Kishtewar, Chumbah, and Palum.

At Runjit's request we mounted the horses he had ordered for us. Baron Hugel, as his principal guest, and Lieutenant Mackeson, as the political agent of the East-India Company, rode two of Runjit's white state horses. I was mounted on a smaller, but very showy, black charger. Our saddles were of crimson and yellow velvet, with golden ornaments, and—as were also the bridles—inlaid with precious stones. We passed down the line of four or five regiments with Runjit, who, from time to time, asked the Baron for his opinion. In the centre was drawn up what is called the Bande-à-casque,—a solid mass of about thirty buglemen, in steel skullcaps, who were blowing with all their might, knowing nothing of music, and making a most horrible din. Runjit halted, that we might listen and admire. It was a moment of severe trial, and might have been worse, had not General Ventura exclaimed, "Ne riez pas, je vous prie, Messieurs!"

We then repaired to Runjit's tents. They were of Kashmirian sulphur-coloured shawl, and their appearance was exceedingly elegant. We sat beside him; and his Sirdars, most splendidly dressed, were standing around. The review then commenced; but I observed nothing remarkable, excepting that the troops, who were formed in squares, with a gun at each angle, in the French fashion, continued to blaze away, without any intermission, for a space of at least six minutes. The elephants, with gold and silver howdahs, were next paraded before the tent; and afterwards came the horses, whose bodies, heads, and necks, were so covered with trappings of gold and jewels, some of the emeralds being very large, that their figure could not well be distinguished. When his favourite horse, Leili, passed us, I heard him remark, that he had cost the lives of four or five thousand men.

I made a sketch afterwards of a large showy grey horse, that was sent to me to be drawn as Leili; but to this day I am not sure that he was the real horse. Runjit's jealousy would prompt him to believe that the King or the East-India Company would ask for him, had they seen his portrait.

On the morning of our departure Runjit presented each of us with a fine horse, a bag of rupees, a gold-mounted sword, belt, and matchlock, an aigrette, and necklace of jewels, several shawls, and other articles,—the Baron's presents being a shade more valuable than mine were.

ORNAMENTS ON MAHMUD'S TOMB, p. 133.

CHAPTER X.

Remarks on Runjit Sing's Conduct and Character—The Girl and Fakir—A Second Anecdote—Mode of Dealing with a Request—Sir H. Fane's Visit to Lahore—His Reception by Runjit—The Bride and Bridegroom—Military Display—Reported Apprehensions of Runjit—Rival Military Practice—Arrival of the Patans—Entertainments—Ladies' Interview with Runjit—Departure of the Commander-in-Chief—The Fakir who buried himself alive—Elephant Fights—The Akalis—Guja Sing and his Invitations.

It was, I think, Mr. Burke who said, that if a man would repeat, as true, what he knew to be untrue, every day for a month, he would believe it in the end; but in spite of such an authority, I much doubt whether the sentence which Runjit has probably uttered, almost mechanically, every day for the last thirty years, "There is great friendship between me and the Company," has had the effect of producing in his mind any real affection, or regard for the British name. I should say, that whilst many rulers have been more ambitious of reputation, few have been more anxious for increase of dominion, than the late Maharajah. A man may be proud of a costly garment, though its weight may be oppressive to him; and Runjit has always been proud of his alliance with the company, though it has always imposed a positive, or indirect, restraint upon his movements. It is not likely, that he should regard the British with any warmer feeling than that of admiration, excited by the superiority which he would vainly hope to attain; and though he may in many instances have evinced a kind esteem for different individuals, yet, on the other hand, his behaviour towards any Englishman, not a Company's servant, who may have crossed the Sutlij with the intention of asking for service, is widely removed from cordiality towards the nation in general. His tyrannical delay of decision, and subsequent withholding of arrears of pay, had to my own knowledge in several instances amounted to cruelty. Runjit caused great misery by similar delay, but he was never fond of shedding blood, while of cunning, he always evinced a sufficient share. M. Court informed me, that when Runjit was a young man, he was often in want of money. Upon one occasion he said he was drowsy without knowing why, sat himself down in a chair, and pretended to sleep for more than half an hour. Circumstances compelled his father, Maha Sing's, ministers to awaken him: they did so, and he told them he had had a dream that troubled him exceedingly; what it was they were bound to enquire, and the more unwilling he appeared to tell it, the more prodigal were they in their offers of consolation and advice. He at last said, that he had dreamed that he had no money to pay his troops, and he had prayed to the Guru, who had appeared to him, and told him to be of good cheer, that if he had no money his friends had, and that he could never remain in want whilst his father's ministers were near him. They were bound to believe the story, and furnished him with the money he wanted, for the honour of having been noticed by the Guru in Runjit's dreams.

Upon another occasion, Runjit had determined to make some one his prisoner.

He accordingly invited him to a friendly conference under a tent, of which the ropes had purposely been loosened. Runjit talked most amicably with him for some time, and then found some pretext for retiring, particularly requesting his guest to remain seated in the tent until his return. The instant he was outside, he gave the signal, and the ropes being cut or unfastened, the tent dropped down upon his astonished friend, whilst Runjit was skipping about from one side to the other, and vowing vengeance upon them, should their carelessness allow such a villain to escape. Runjit's practical jokes were never remarkable for refinement; and when he took a whim into his head, he cared not a rush for appearances, and never thought of consequences. Olim, appotus, animi laxandi causâ, desuper ab elephante in capita circumstantis turbæ mingere aliquando solitus est. He had fallen in love with a dancing-girl, and forthwith she became his favorite. Her brother, or pretended brother, was a sword-grinder in Lahore, and he was quickly promoted to all honor. He rode upon an elephant, and was attended by a guard. He became far too great a man to look down upon the street before him, and soon ran his elephant over a fakir of great sanctity, who died in consequence of the injuries he received. Runjit, however, cared for none of these things, so long as he enjoyed himself; but in order to force him to take notice of what had passed, the fakir's brethren placed a building to his memory, on one of the highest mounds amongst the ruins at Lahore, in order that Runjit might see it whenever he rode that way. This had the desired effect; Runjit appeased the fakirs, by dismissing the girl, having, it is probable become tired of her company; and the sword-grinder was disgraced at the same time.

I am not sure, whether it was the same or another favourite dancing-girl, who one day tied his hands together, most likely at his own request, she thinking it, no doubt, an excellent joke to have done so. Runjit then sent in a hurry for two of his Sirdars, Rajah Dhihan Sing, and Kosheal Sing, the Jemadar or chief captain; who rapidly obeyed the summons, thinking that business of importance was to be discussed, and feigned the greatest horror at seeing their master with his hands tied. Runjit then asked them, what punishment ought to be inflicted upon the person, who had dared to tie his hands? A heavy fine! was the reply; and Runjit made the girl refund to him several thousand of his rupees for her temerity; all of which, and more with them, she was quite sure of receiving again afterwards; and Runjit then got fifty thousand rupees apiece from his two Sirdars, for the honour of untying him.

By persevering in my request, Runjit at length allowed me to attempt his portrait in full durbar. When I first asked him I was at Lahore, in company with Baron Hugel. He coloured, smiled, and replied, "To-morrow, at Amritsir!" which was only an oriental mode of refusing, as he had no idea of going to Amritsir. I again respectfully urged the request, "No! No!" he said, "I am an old man. Take his picture," pointing to Heera Sing; "he is young and handsome." This, however, I never did, as it would have looked too much like flattery to his master. Had I been obsequious enough to have given Runjit two eyes, he would probably have made no objection; and when he did sit to me, he was constantly turning away, so as to conceal his blind side.

There was scarcely any of the Sirdars around him, whom one would not have been glad to have pillaged in the dark; so bedizened were they generally with gold and jewels, pearls, emeralds, and the rubies of Budukshan. It would be absurd and illiberal not to make allowances for the want of education; but otherwise, I should say, that taken as a body, the Sikh Sirdars, of whom the durbar of Lahore was composed, might generally, with some little exception, be designated as gentlemen blackguards, and "something more," to whom a disregard of principle, subtle intrigue, and calm hypocrisy, were alike familiar and diurnal. Each of them was a party in himself, and would have been rejoiced to see his neighbour ruined and in disgrace. Runjit had made the fortunes of many of them—he has been known, when in his cups, to boast of having done so;—and a feeling of gratitude, it may be presumed, combined with the sense to appreciate the superior powers of intellect that remained, whilst his body was enfeebled, instructed them to avoid the risk of an open quarrel with each other, and to place out of sight for a time their mutual distrust, jealousy, and differences, in the full persuasion that it was for their real interest to do so, and that all would be well with them whilst they still allowed themselves to be guided and controlled by his master spirit. I do not believe them to be remarkable for personal courage. A year or two ago, General Ventura, nettled at something that had passed, told Runjit in full durbar, that his Sirdars were all cowards, or used words to that effect. They immediately rose in a fury and gathered round him, and Runjit himself, old and enfeebled, leaped from his chair in an ungovernable passion, called for his sword and shield, and told the General to draw and defend himself; whilst Ventura, a sabreur of Wagram, looked round upon the gathered storm with a coolness that showed he did not expect a practical refutation of what he had just asserted; and then both pacified and pleased the Maharajah by saying that he was his servant, that his life was his if he wished for it, but that come what would, he would never draw his sword against his king and master.

Sir Henry Fane, the commander-in-chief, crossed the Sutlij at Hurree-ke-Putun (the green ferry), on the 3rd of March, 1837. It was at a very early hour on a cold misty morning, that I repaired, in company with Captain Wade, whose guest I was, to the presence of Shere Sing, who with Lena Sing, a Sirdar of rank and family, and the most learned man in the Punjab, had been deputed by Runjit, to receive and attend upon his Excellency. We found him seated in his tent on the banks of the river, surrounded by his guards and richly-liveried attendants; and after the usual complimentary conversation, he, or some one near him, asked if there were any very strong men with the commander-in-chief, and pointing to a gigantic Sikh who was sitting near him, proceeded seriously to intimate, that he would be ready for a trial of strength with any one of them who would favour him with a contest. We were amused with this antediluvian idea of what a commander-in-chief or his men ought to be.

The river, just joined by the Beas, including its shoals and islands, was, if I rightly remember, considerably more than a mile in width from one bank to another; it was covered with large boats, whose dark outlines, and that of the military objects they contained, were alone discernible: colour could not be distinguished on account of the mist, and the whole scene would have formed an admirable subject for the pencil of a Rysdael. Sir Henry was too quick for Shere Sing, and had mounted his horse in the Punjab, whilst we were still with Shere Sing in his tent, who was waiting until he should be informed that the commander-in-chief's boat was approaching the bank.

On the sixth at day break, the commander-in-chief and his staff were met, as they were approaching Amritsir, by the Jemadar (or chief captain) Kosheal Sing, and Rajah Dhihan Sing. The handsome person and appearance of the latter, was strikingly distinguished; his costume was half Sikh, half European; and the gorgeous colours of his national dress were seen to greater advantage by being contrasted with a splendid French cuirass, presented to him, I believe, by General Allard, who had just then returned from Europe. The *cortége* was subsequently met by the Kunwur Khuruk Sing, as heir-apparent, who conducted his guests to within a short distance from the Ram-Bagh, or garden of Ramah, within which Runjit had passed the night, whence, after giving him a salute of twenty-one guns, Sir Henry returned to the camp. After breakfast every one sallied forth to be present at the Malakât, or meeting. We again approached the garden, under a salute to the commander, from the Maharajah's guns placed there. Numerous elephants in gorgeous trappings, presenting to the eye a moving confusion of cloth of gold, yellow, green, and crimson-coloured silks, were shortly seen to issue from the portals of the Ram-Bagh. As they approached us, Runjit's elephant was pushed forward in advance of the others :

[1] O qualis facies et quali digna tabellâ,
Cum Gætula ducem portaret bellua luscum!
Juvenal, Sat. X.

I saw the blood mount into his face, and his eye glisten intensely with the pride and satisfaction which he felt at such a moment. Sir Henry received him with a cordial English shake of the hand, and was conducted by Runjit to the tent prepared for his reception. Here there were nearly sixty elephants in attendance, drawn or disposed in different lines. After the usual compliments had passed on both sides, Runjit ordered his favourite horses to be exhibited: they were fine animals of their kind, and richly caparisoned, and pranced, caracoled, and curvetted to admiration, but seemed better fitted to draw a state

[1] This apt quotation was sported upon the occasion by my friend M. P Edgworth, Esq., of Umbala, who was present.

carriage, than to go across country: they were chiefly of the Duni breed. Duni is, I believe, a district on the eastern bank of the Indus, to the south of Attok. Runjit has four hundred brood mares, either there or in other parts of the Punjab. We afterwards departed, Runjit standing at the place of egress, and shaking hands with every one as he passed. On the afternoon of the same day, the commander-in-chief was again invited to the residence of the young and royal bridegroom. The interview was enlivened by the performances of the dancing girls. The Maharajah, and No Nehal Sing, who was half covered with a golden veil, were seated under a tree, loaded with artificial oranges. Presents of money, to the amount, I think, of eleven thousand rupees, (eleven hundred pounds,) were presented to the commander-in-chief. The crowd in the city was intense, the streets exceedingly narrow, the dust and heat intolerable, and the wild tumult was not a little increased by the incessant roar of Runjit's guns, a few of which were so placed—no doubt by his own order, for he always enjoyed a joke—as to be discharged under the very trunks of the elephants, which, when the meeting was over, we had the greatest difficulty in regaining.

On the eighth the camp moved to Atari, the residence of the bride's father; whose castle, presenting a collection of flat roofs and square and windowless turrests, arose with some majesty on the left of the encampment. A grand procession was arranged for the afternoon. Artificial parterres, temples, towers, and whirligigs, were carried along with it. Music was playing, and cannon firing. Thousands of natives were threading their way through the crowded elephants; and ran the greatest risk of being trampled upon, in the attempt to pick up the rupees which were distributed, right and left, from those in advance. The Maharajah held his levee on a raised terrace, commanding a fine view of the plain. No Nehal Sing again wore his veil of gold, and the dancing-girls were again called into requisition. In the evening there was an exhibition of fireworks, the castle was splendidly illuminated, and Runjit conducted his guests along a broad way, lined with his troops, blazing with artificial light, and extending for several hundred yards from the castle to the camp.

On the ninth commenced the most extraordinary part of the scene. In honour of his distinguished guest, Runjit had ordered a small rupee (about one shilling and sixpence) to be given to those who would receive it; and, in order to prevent any one from asking for it a second time, he had directed a large space of ground to be enclosed, whose circumference could not have been less than between two and three miles. There were eighty doorways or openings in the enclosure; and, at each of them, was stationed an officer, to superintend the distribution of the money. There could not have been less than four laks, i. e. four hundred thousand persons collected together; and many of these were the venders of water, salt, flour, firewood, and other necessaries of life. In the three days that elapsed in liberating such a crowd, Runjit must have paid away upwards of thirty thousand pounds in this manner.

The Commander-in-chief was then conducted to view the presents made by the bride, or rather by her father, to the young and royal bridegroom. These consisted of eleven elephants, one hundred and one horses, with numerous camels, cows, and buffaloes; and the ingenuity of the Sikh artistes had been taxed to provide a fitting quantity of the most approved sweetmeats and confectionery. The space of not much less than an acre was nearly covered with female attire, and a brilliant display of the rich silks of Multan, and the golden and scarlet kimkab of Benares; and on some ropes, that had been stretched across them, were suspended a large collection of the less gaudy, but more chastely-coloured, shawls from the unrivalled looms of Kashmir.

The place allotted to the Commander-in-chief's camp at Lahore was finely situated on the north of the city. It was, in fact, on the edge of the parade-ground. The north side of the camp was washed by the tranquil stream of the Ravi, four or five hundred yards in width. On the opposite bank towered the lofty minarets of Shah

Dhera, or the tomb of Jehan Guire; and, in the furthest verge of the horizon, were distinctly visible, particularly at day-break, the snowy summits of the Pir Panjal range, thirteen thousand five hundred feet high, separating Kashmir from the plains of the Punjab.

The time at Lahore was occupied by a succession of visits, fêtes, and reviews. On the fourteenth, the Commander-in-chief's escort was inspected. It consisted of a squadron of His Majesty's sixteenth lancers, under the command of Major Cuerton, and another of native lancers; ten companies of infantry, and six pieces of horse-artillery, under the command of Captains Timbrel and Timings. Runjit was particularly delighted with the general appearance of the troops, and the scientific combination of movements exhibited by the cavalry, infantry, and artillery together. His Excellency explained to him the reasons for each manœuvre, he being perhaps the only native of the Punjab who could properly understand them; and at last he could refrain no longer, but, turning to Captain Wade, who was acting as interpreter, remarked, with energy of manner, "My Sirdars tell me that this discipline is all nonsense, and would be useless in action: what fools they are!"

In nothing has Runjit shown his prudence and depth of judgment more, than in his determined refusal to listen to the advice of the little great ones of his court, who are constantly urging him to oppose the wishes of the Indian Government. Rajah Dhihan Sing once went so far as to call him a "woman" to his face. This was, I think, when he was prevented from marching upon Sinde, in 1836-7; and when, as a punning friend remarked, he thought himself "a man more sinned against than sinning," in making his preparations. He is much indebted to his French officers for the truth upon these occasions. The besieged Bhurtporeans tried to bribe him to advance. He is said to have consulted with General Ventura on the chance of success, if he made an attack upon Lodiana. The General replied, that he was his servant, and was ready to obey his orders; but advised him to think again before he ran such a risk of losing the Punjab. When the Bhurtporeans found that their attempts at bribery, as detailed in Captain Osborne's account, were unavailing, they sent him a woman's dress.

A gun was purposely dismounted and set up again, in less than half a minute. Runjit and the Sikhs were much surprized; but they could not, at first, be persuaded that the carriage was not out of repair. The gun should have been dropped when at a gallop, and the effect would then have been electrical.

The fifteenth of March was the day appointed for the return visit of Runjit to the Commander-in-chief, in his Excellency's tent. Rajah Dhihan Sing stood behind his master's chair. After the usual compliments, Runjit assured Sir Henry that he looked upon him in the same light as the Governor-general, and that between two such illustrious friends he drew no distinction. He asked his opinion as to the relative merits of the armies of the three Presidencies, and as to Sir Henry's early history as a soldier; and added, that he himself, during a campaign, had frequently divided his last bit of bread with his own Sepahis. Many of the officers present were then separately introduced to him.

During the interview a slight tittering was commenced by some of the Sikh attendants, in a dark corner of the tent. They had detected the presence of some of the ladies of the escort, who were endeavouring to catch a glimpse of the assembly through an opening in the top of the cloth that formed the walls of the tent. Rajah Sucheyt Sing with all the impertinence of ultra dandyism, was gradually sidling up the passage out of the tent, in the hope, no doubt, of seeing or being seen by them; but Lieutenant Mackeson, the assistant political agent, disconcerted him exceedingly, by gently taking him by the arm, and quietly walking him back again.

When the visit was over, Runjit, whose head reached up to Sir Henry Fane's waist, was conducted by him into an inner tent, where the presents, consisting of shawls, fire-arms, &c., were laid out for his inspection. Several fine horses, either imported from England, or stud-bred (that is, reared at one of the Company's breeding establishments in Bengal), were paraded and given to him. Presents of rifles, pistols, and other articles, were given to his principal Sirdars; and he took leave, highly pleased with his visit. The cavalry of the escort were drawn up close to the tent. Runjit, who was always fond of fun, and, moreover, would never let slip so fair an opportunity of testing the training of their horses, purposely ran his elephants along the line, and within about a foot of their heads. A young horse regards an elephant with peculiar terror, as was exemplified by an artillery-horse opposite to them, that reared, plunged, and struggled to extricate himself; but Fabricius himself, aided by his reason, could not have displayed a more stoical indifference, or remained more motionless, than the well-broken chargers of the lancers.

In Prinsep's Life of Runjit Sing we read that he was scarcely able to dismiss from his mind the idea of treacherous behaviour towards him, on the part of Lord William Bentinck, at Rupur; and that, in the middle of the night preceding his first interview with the Governor-general, he sent for General Allard, and was scarcely satisfied by his offer of staking his own life upon the safety of his master; and that the astrologers, after consulting the Gurunth, advised him to take with him a present of two apples, and to judge of the sincerity of his welcome by the manner in which they were received. Although experience and his own penetration may have secured him from fears of a similar nature upon the present occasion, yet it would appear that suspicions of foul play towards him were still rife in the minds of his attendants. Pindi Dos, was, I think, the name of one of the Bhais, or "brothers," for so the servants at the royal palace were designated, who was kindly sent by Runjit to attend upon me, when, in the beginning of the last year, I travelled into Kishtewar, Budrawar, and Chumbah; and, in fact, made my way directly through the mountains from Kashmir to Lodiana. This man assured me, that he and his brethren had agreed amongst themselves, that, at the interview I have just described, they would force their way as far into the tent as possible, so as not to lose sight of their master for a moment; and that their fears for his safety had taken such a possession of their minds, that they had packed up, and even sent away, his most valuable effects, in order that, if they succeeded in the rescue, the wish to preserve them might not induce him to linger behind. I do not answer for the truth of this story, but am myself inclined to believe it; as there was certainly, at first, a considerable disturbance at the door of the tent, created by the Sikh attendants, who wished to enter it; and my informant, moreover, was one of the most respectable men in the Maharajah's service, and could have had no motive for misrepresentation.

The Sikh Sepahis do not wear gaiters; and instead of a cap or helmet of any sort, a red cloth is rolled up, and twisted through and over their hair, so as to form a turban, for the Sikhs do not shave the head like the Hindus, and when seen on parade at some little distance, they are scarcely to be distinguished from the Company's troops. The officers are allowed to exercise their own taste in dress, and accordingly every one turns out better or worse, according to his esprit de corps, his personal vanity, and the length of his purse. "Voilà une grâce Punjabienne!" exclaimed M. Court, as he pointed out to us a Sikh officer who was passing in review, in front of his battalion, and thought he had hit it exactly, by buttoning back one of the lappels of his coat, in order to display the bosom of a clean white shirt. One day Runjit exhibited a line of twenty-three thousand disciplined troops, and as the commander-in-chief passed along the lines, he was saluted with "God save the King," from the drums and fifes of each brigade. The manœuvring and appearance of the regiments, commanded by the French officers, called forth his unqualified approval.

The British Artillery practice was very successful, and the shrapnell told with tremendous effect upon the curtain. Runjit, as usual, stuck up his red silk chattah, or umbrella, which, after two or three shots, was rendered utterly useless. It was first struck, I believe, by Lieut. Mackenzie, of the Lodiana troop. The Sikhs, whose artillery did not shine, were detected loading a gun with grape, in order to make sure of hitting it, after having failed with their round shot. It was ascertained by experiment, that the Company's powder carried one-third further than Runjit's.

But perhaps the most interesting exhibition was that of the Ghoracheras, or irregular horse. Runjit received the Commander-in-chief and his suite at one of the Bara Deris, or summer-houses, on the parade ground; and the Ghoracheras cantered by in single file. There were many hundreds of them in yellow scarfs, tunics, and plumed turbans, armed with pistols, swords, and other accoutrements. Nothing could be more picturesque, than to see one of these grey-bearded veterans come up at a canter, with a long spear or matchlock in his bridle hand, and, reining in his Rosinante for a moment, turn towards the Maharajah, throw down a piece of money as a token of homage to his old chief and companion in arms, and give him loudly, and emphatically, the national salutation of "Wah! Guru-Gee-Ke-Futi!" (may the Guru give you the victory,) then set stirrups to his horse's side, the pointed heel of the stirrup forming the spur, and dart forward to make room for another Ghorachera, as martial and wild-looking as himself. Runjit was certainly never much given to the pathetic: I have heard one of his French officers describe him as a man without passion; but I have been credibly informed, that he has been seen to weep as some of his old soldiers have approached him with a petition, and shewed their wounds as they presented it.

Pir Mohamed Khan, brother of Dost Mahomed Khan, of Kabul, had thought fit to fly from the presence of his brother, and consult his own safety by a shameful desertion to the side of Runjit. It was, no doubt, by a pre-concerted arrangement, that he and his *cortége*, consisting of about a dozen retainers, approached during the inspection, to make their salaams for the first time They were all well armed, and covered with dust. Pir Mohamed Khan, a very fat man, wore a steel scull-cap, and a coat of chain-mail. They dismounted, and Runjit and his Sirdars rose to receive them, and gave them a cordial welcome. Runjit coloured, talked, laughed, chuckled, and pulled his own beard incessantly, as he was accustomed to do when much pleased. He could not conceal the delight and satisfaction he felt, because the Patans had arrived at a moment when his distinguished visitors were sitting beside him, and witnessing what he conceived to be a triumph over his enemy, Dost Mohamed Khan. Pir Mohamed Khan was not the less welcome, that he had brought with him, amongst other presents, a horse called the Koh-i-nur, or mountain of light, of which Runjit had heard, and had long wished to be the possessor. I had seen the horse at Kabul, and shewn the Maharajah a sketch of him; and when he was brought out before him, he was so fearful of being deceived, that he sent for me, to come and assure him that it really was the same horse. The Koh-i-nur was of a fine grey colour, and in England would have been considered as a neat looking horse, three-parts bred, and up to about thirteen stone as a hunter.

Nothing could exceed the kindness of the French and Italian general officers, M. M. Allard, Court, Ventura, and Avetabile, during the whole time of the Commander-in-chief's visit: they seemed to vie with each other in the performance of polite attentions to the Maharajah's guests; and Generals Ventura and Allard gave a splendid entertainment to the Commander-in-chief a short time before his departure. Some of the principal Sirdars were invited in the evening, and came in anxious expectation of seeing the English ladies dance, who, it was understood, were going to perform a quadrille, or a waltz, in order that they might be able to say that they had danced at Lahore. The Sirdars, however, were disappointed, as it was very properly considered inexpedient to indulge their curiosity in this particular. Perhaps they thought it very singular that the ladies were not commanded to dance, whether they were willing or not, as an officer, who was on duty at the court of a Rajah, on the Indus, told me that he was seriously asked, if it were not true that Lord William Bentinck, when at Rupur, had made his lady nach, *i. e.*, dance, for the amusement of Runjit.

At a party, given either by the Commander-in-chief or Captain Wade, Shere Singh and Rajah Sucheyt Sing took their seats at table, not to eat, for it would have been against their religion to do so, but to see and be seen. Shere Sing wore nothing but a plain white scarf and tunic, and did, I believe, eat a little, whilst Rajah Sucheyt Sing, a Hindu by birth, and possessing all the prejudices of a Hindu, sat in state during the whole of dinner time, the "observed of all observers," and covered with magnificent jewels, most innocently inhaling the fumes of a fine piece of stewed beef, close to which, by mere accident, he happened to be seated. Vilayuti huren, "European venison," is the name under which beef is usually concealed from a Hindu, and pork from the more inquisitive Mussulman.

I must not forget to mention, that the ladies were permitted to visit the mother of the Kunwur Khuruk Sing, and that the return visit of Sir Henry Fane to the Prince himself, was perhaps the most uninteresting interview that took place at Lahore.

On the eighteenth of March, Runjit gave a party in the palace to the ladies of the escort. He sat in his chair as usual, with one foot uncovered. An even number is thought unlucky, and odd numbers, such as eleven, fifty-one, one hundred and one, or eleven thousand, are always preferred, when the amount of a present, or the fortunate hour is under consideration. In making a present, an even number is looked upon as too decisive in its effects, and as emblematical of a wish to have done with an existing friendship, or compact; whilst an odd one is considered as leaving it in existence and unfinished, and certain, though undefined. Thus the wedding presents of the royal bride were in odd numbers, as being more lucky; and

Runjit now sat with one foot unstockinged, in the belief, that nothing which could pass in the course of conversation would be unsusceptible of change, and that he thus secured to himself some undefinable path for the access of good fortune, and means of escape from a suspicious result. There were present, Miss Fane, Mrs. Fane, Mrs. Torrens, Mrs. and Miss Churchill, Mrs. Bere, and Mrs. Van Cortlandt, a lady married to an officer in the Punjab. They were separately introduced to Runjit, who shook hands with them. Shere Sing sat in a chair, nearly opposite to the Maharajah: on his right were the Commander-in-chief and the ladies; and on his left, sat No Nehal Sing, and Hera Sing. The dancing girls were singing in front. Nothing, I believe, took place beyond the ordinary run of conversation, but it was amusing to watch the two last-mentioned personages. They gazed at the ladies, as if they had never seen them before, and would never see them again, their eyes being fairly rivetted upon them during the whole interview; and I think it more than probable, that No Nehal Sing did not bestow a single thought upon his young bride whilst it lasted.

Runjit, who had himself drawn up the prospectus of the manner in which each day was to be occupied, had added a few more to be passed in what he called "friendly conferences;" but, as the hot weather was rapidly advancing, it was considered advisable not to remain longer at Lahore. The festival of the Houli was celebrated on the twenty-second. The presents to the officers, consisting of shawls, gold bracelets, swords, and matchlocks,—all of which were afterwards seized by the political agent on behalf of the Company,—were given at the parting interview, which took place, I think, on the twenty-eighth; and before the end of the month, the Commander-in-chief had recrossed the Sutlij at Ferozpore, and was in full march for Simla.

I saw a good deal of the fakir, or jogi, who buries himself, in a sitting posture, for days, weeks, or months; and was within one march of Lahore, on my return from Kabul, when he was unkennelled, in the presence of the Maharajah, Captain Wade, and Dr. Mc Gregor; and I could easily have galloped forward in time to see the ceremony, had I been informed of what was going to take place. His countenance was expressive of extreme cunning; and I once heard him coolly say that he was five hundred years old, and give the most absurd accounts of his methods of preparation, some of which are detailed by Captain Osborne and Lieutenant Boileau.

In Wilson's sketch of the religious ceremonies of the Hindus, we read that the term Jogi, or Yogi, is properly applicable to the followers of the Yoga or Pajantala school of philosophy; who maintain the possibility of acquiring, even in life, entire command over elementary matter, by means of certain ascetic privations. It is sufficient to observe, that these practices consist of long-continued suppression of respiration, of inhaling or exhaling the breath in a particular manner, sitting in eighty-four different attitudes, fixing the eyes on the top of the nose; and in endeavouring, by such abstinence, to effect an union, for so the word "yoga" signifies, between a portion of vital spirit residing in the body, and that which pervades all nature, and is identical with Siva, considered as the superior being, and the source and essence of all creation. When this mystic union is effected, the Yogi is liberated from his living body, and regains an entire command over all worldly substances. He can make himself lighter than the lightest substances, heavier than the heaviest; can become as vast, or as minute, as he pleases; can traverse all space; can animate any dead body, by transferring his spirit into it from his own; can render himself invisible; can attain all objects; become equally acquainted with the past, present, and future; and be finally united with Siva; and, consequently, exempted, like the rest of mankind, from being born again upon earth.

In the Ayeen Akberi, vol. ii. p. 445, we find, that with regard to sitting in eighty-four different ways, it is remarked, that the author has seen many who practise the austerities of the "assum," or sitting, and has been astonished how they can make their muscles, nerves, and bones, so obedient to their command. Some of them could hold their breath for an incredible length of time.

In the Asiatic Monthly Journal for March, 1829, we find the following account of the Brahmin who sat upon air. "A Brahmin, old and slightly made, reported to be of high caste, contrives to poise himself in a most extraordinary manner in the air. The only apparatus seen was a piece of plank, which, with four pegs, he forms into a kind of long stool. Upon this, in a little brass saucer or socket, he places, in a perpendicular position, a hollow bamboo; over which he puts a kind of crutch, like the top of a walking-crutch, covering it with a piece of common hide. These materials he carries with him in a little bag, which is shown to those who come to see him exhibit. The servants of the house hold a blanket before him; and, when it is withdrawn, he is discovered poised in the air about four feet from the ground, in a sitting attitude, the outer edge of one hand merely touching the crutch, the fingers of that hand deliberately counting his beads, and the other hand and arm in an erect position. The blanket was then held up before him, and a gurgling noise was heard, like that occasioned by wind escaping from a bladder or tube, and when the screen was withdrawn he was again standing on *terra firma*. The same man has a power of remaining under water for several hours. He only said that he was accustomed to it. He remained poised in air for twelve minutes, in the presence of the person who gave this account; but, before the Governor of Madras, he continued on his baseless seat for forty minutes."

After thus knowing what the Jogi believes himself capable of doing, and actually can do, there is no difficulty in understanding how the natives of India can be completely deceived by appearances. It is not to be denied, that every European who has been present at the opening of the innermost box, in which the fakir sat, of whom I am speaking, has been staggered, for the time at least, into a belief of the reality and truth of his pretensions. His whole appearance has been that of a sitting corpse, excepting that there appears to be a swelling over the entire scalp. When hot water and the hot cake has been applied, this swelling has gradually disappeared, and he recovered, as if his whole life had been collected on the top of his head. After the Commander-in-chief had quitted Lahore, I obtained a promise from Runjit that the fakir should be allowed to cross the Sutlij and visit Simla, where I engaged that he should be very handsomely rewarded; but the Rajah Dhihan

Sing ordered him off in a contrary direction the next morning. Previously to this, Dr. Wood, staff-surgeon to the Commander-in-chief, who had been left behind at Lahore at the particular request of Runjit, and myself had offered him a very handsome reward, if he would allow us to bury him only for a week or ten days; but he constantly refused to accede to our request, although he had the Maharajah's permission to trust himself with us. Runjit seemed to enjoy the joke, remarking that the fakir would find it difficult to deceive us.

In the Quarterly Oriental Magazine, March and June, 1824, p. 60, it is stated, that in the thirty-fifth of Akber's reign, it was said of Sheik Kamal Biabani, that he possessed the power of transporting himself to a distance; so that a person who talked with him on one side of the river would, upon crossing to the other, be again saluted with his voice. Akber went to see him, and offered his whole kingdom if he would instruct him to do so likewise. He refused; and Akber ordered him to be tied hand and foot, and that he should be tossed into the river, if he refused to give him the information he wanted. Upon this the man confessed that he acted in concert with his son, who was on the opposite side of the river, and counterfeited his father's voice. Had Runjit really believed the pretensions of the fakir, he would have acted like Akber, and have ordered him to bury himself, guarding him in good earnest; but he was sceptical, and death and detection might then have followed. The destruction too of a very holy man would have been attributed to Runjit; who would, moreover, have deprived himself of a powerful hold over the minds of his subjects, by upsetting the pretensions of all other fakirs whatsoever to a preternatural power of any kind, inasmuch as they could hardly have been ever equal to those of this man. I do not think that his mere refusal to be buried under English surveillance can be fairly regarded as conclusive evidence of his being an impostor. A native would be so suspicious as to find it difficult to divest himself of the idea that some foul play would prevent his success; and I think it will be admitted, that the mere fact of his allowing himself to be shut up at all, is sufficiently astonishing. The air he inhaled must have been rapidly deprived of its oxygen; and any concentrated nourishment he may have concealed in his mouth must soon have been exhausted. We must either, then, conclude that he received, by means of pipes, a supply of both these necessaries, or that, in conformity with appearances, he had found out the means of assuming and remaining in a state of suspended animation. The greatest proof of his being an impostor is, I think, that he affirms the length of time he may be buried to be quite immaterial, and that the functions of his body are equally capable of restoration whether he be entombed for ten months or ten days; but, at the same time, it is clear that the falsity of such an assertion can never be fairly tested, in the face of existing appearances, until he be locked up with a guard that can be depended upon, and the right of inspection at any time, without public notice, be reserved to his employers. We may suppose any thing,—that he receives a supply of nourishment; that he is released by his friends, and replaced in his confinement; and that, when the time for his exhumation arrives, he may render himself inanimate with narcotics;—but no one can say that appearances are not, as yet, stronger than probabilities; and though I believe him, as I have said, to be an impostor to a certain extent, yet I certainly think he is in possession of a trick worth knowing, be it what it may.

As I intended to try and reach the source of the western branch of the Indus in the same year, I remained at Lahore, for the purpose of getting permission to pass again through Kashmir, in my way to Little Tibet.

During the interval, I enjoyed the agreeable society of Dr. Wood, already mentioned. No man could possibly bestow more attention upon his patient; but it was doubtful if Runjit ever took any part of the prescribed medicines, although he would go through the farce of sending the fakir Aziz-ud-Dyn, who was his physician in ordinary, as well as secretary of state, to see them prepared and made up. Runjit left Lahore, and moved his camp to Ram-Nagur, on the banks of the Chenab, about eighteen miles, I forget the exact distance, below Vizirabad; and our mornings there were passed in a very amusing manner. The Maharajah never, at any place, took a ride without being attended by elephants, bearing his tents, bed, cooking utensils, and full camp equipage; and here he himself, as well as every one with him, was either on horseback, or in his palanquin, before day break; and, to use a common phrase, "there was always something going on." The artillery practice was worth seeing, because it was so infamously bad. The elephant fights were less so than might be imagined; two of these animals were driven at each other, by their respective mahouts or riders; and after a struggle, in which brute strength, without the least quickness or activity, was brought into play, one of them succeeded in fixing his tusks in such a manner about the head of the other, that he was enabled fairly to lift him off his hind legs: the other, thus defeated, became outrageous, and still goaded onward by his mahout, strode furiously over the plain, dispersing the galloping crowd, giving chase to the horsemen, many of whom contended for the honour of running a greater risk, by riding nearer to him, than another. In going out or returning in the morning, the Maharajah would occasionally be annoyed by persons suddenly rising out of the ground under his horse's head; they had petitions to present, or complaints to make; and unable to approach him in the crowd, had adopted the very knowing plan of digging a large hole by the side of the road, and concealing themselves in it till Runjit approached them.

Galloping at speed with a drawn sword, and cutting a lota, or brass pot, on the ground, in passing, was a feat more difficult, I suspect, than it appeared to be: young No Nehal Sing performed it better than any one else. We saw a Sikh start off at speed, with one foot in the stirrup, the wooden projection in front of the saddle tightly grasped in one hand, and thus supported, he so lowered himself that he could have reached any thing upon the ground with the other; and at a word from Runjit, the two brother Rajahs, Dhihan and Sucheyt Sing, rode off together, and discharged their matchlocks at each other, whilst at full gallop.

A tent peg was driven into the ground, and the Ghoracheras, one by one, rode at it with a spear, at full gallop, and some of them succeeded in striking it with the point, and forcing it out of the ground, cheering wildly as they carried it off.

One morning it was intimated to Sultan Mohamed Khan, the deposed chief of Peshawur, and Pir Mohamed Khan, whom I have already noticed, that they should exhibit with their spears. Accordingly, a man was placed in a convenient situation, holding an orange covered with gold leaf, on his open and extended palm. The Patan chiefs and their attendants rode at this one by one, at full gallop, and took it off the man's hand, with the point of the spear, in the most beautiful style imaginable, not missing it in one single instance. So loud were we in our praises, that Runjit, by whose side we were standing, grew, I thought, a little jealous, and said "Enough!" sooner than he otherwise might have done.

The Akalis, or Sikh fanatic priests, though considerably reduced in number, are so much respected by the people, that their power is still not to be despised. They had some complaints to make about this time, and became so outrageous, that Runjit increased the strength of his guard, and two cannon loaded with grape were constantly ready for them. At last Runjit appointed a morning, on which he said he would inspect and enlist such among them as he thought fit. We rode to his tent, which was pitched on a plain away from the main camp. Here we found a large guard, and the Akalis ranged in line within, about sixty yards off, and opposite to him. They were called up one by one, their horses and arms were inspected; some were rejected, and others enrolled amongst his Goracheras. All was going on very quietly, when suddenly, a person with a petition attempted to cross the ranks of the Akalis from behind, and ran towards the Maharajah. The man was immediately seized, and but a slight disturbance created. Runjit was evidently frightened, probably thinking that the Akalis were going to rush in upon him; but without waiting to ascertain from what cause the noise really proceeded, he started up on the instant, hurried to the door of his tent, and asked for his horse. He had the presence of mind, however, to pause for an moment, by way of saving appearances, before he mounted, and made some remarks upon one of the led horses that always attended his *cortège*, and then returned to his own Bara Deri, without having finished the morning's work.

Whilst we were encamped at Ramnagur, Dr. Wood and myself received invitations from poor Guja Sing, already noticed at the commencement of this volume. He had returned from his mission to Calcutta, with an anglomania upon him. He wore an English general officer's uniform, and rode about, contrary to the custom of persons of rank in these countries, either alone, or with but very few attendants. His notes to us were written in Persian, upon English gold-edged pink paper. My own, literally translated, ran nearly as follows:

"Kind and dear Friend! may his friendship be increased!

"After the expression of an ardent wish for a meeting, which (wish) like your virtues, has no limit: it is made known to your excellent understanding, that, praise be to God! the rose-bud of mutual welfare is expanding in the garden of intimate friendship. My friend! it has been my wish, that a personal interview might be accomplished, under the happy auspices of friends; and this day, Friday, at half-past four o'clock, my friends, the English gentlemen, will confer upon me the honour of a visit in my tent. I therefore trouble you with a request, that, looking upon this abode as entirely your own, you will honour it with your presence at the time above-mentioned. What (can I say) more ?"

We accepted the invitation, expecting, after the pink note paper, to find a sumptuous repast in the Calcutta style, and a nach, consisting of half-a-dozen dancing girls at least. Instead of these, we saw a single, but very good performer, on the native guitar. A dinner, which we found had been entirely dressed by our own servants, in our own dishes ; while Guja Sing, and two or three friends, sat at a respectful distance, and talked to us during the repast, more apparently for the pleasure of seeing us eat, than for the sake of our good company.

EMPEROR BABER'S TOMB, AT KABUL.—p. 200.

CHAPTER XI.

Afghan Music—History of Haji Khan—The ruling Afghan Families—Actions of Dost Mohamed Khan—Rokya Begum—Feuds among the Chiefs—Dost Mohamed becomes Master of Kabul—Wins over Haji Khan—Patan Character—Person of Dost Mohamed—His Durbar—Address—A Mullah's Interruption—The Court of Runjit Sing—Comparison—Officers of the Ameer—Dialects in use at Kabul—Mohamed Akber Khan—Dost Mohamed's Children and Family—Simple Food—Dress—Portrait Painting—Dost Mohamed's Horses—Bigotry of the Mullahs—Character of Dost Mohamed—Morals of Kabul—Revenue—Justice—Armed Forces.

A WORD on the Afghan music.—One evening at Kabul, the Nawab, Jabar-

Khan, sent for me to hear his singers, and a most uproarious noise they made. There were six or seven men screaming at the top of their voices, with an accompaniment of native violins, guitars, finger-drums, and small cymbals. Haji Khan, Dost Mohamed's commander of cavalry, came in, and I was introduced to him. The life of Haji Baba is no caricature; and I subjoin the life of Haji Khan to show through what extraordinary circumstances a man may rise to eminence in the East. Of his early life I have heard nothing, excepting that he was a Kashmirian by birth, and that his father was a shawl merchant. Haji Khan started on a pilgrimage to Mecca. He has been heard to say, that while wandering in Arabia he was so destitute, that when an old woman wished to give him some dates, he had nothing to wrap them up in. Upon his return eastward he engaged himself as a soldier in the service of Sheyn Khan, a servant of Mustafa Khan, a chief of Beluchistan; and soon became distinguished by his bravery. Sheyn Khan called him and treated him as his brother. When Sheyn Khan left Mustafa Khan's service, and entered that of the Nawab Jabar Khan, Haji gained favour with the Nawab, who took him into his own service. He afterwards went with Futi Khan to the Persian war, and was wounded in the engagement which took place when they penetrated beyond Mushid, where the Afghans were beaten by Hussein-Ali Mirza. Kamran of Herat wished him to enter his service, and Haji Khan was brought before him on a sick bed; but he refused, and fled from Herat to Kandahar, into the service of Shere Dil Khan, and attended him on his expedition against Kabul. He then commenced intriguing with Dost Mohamed Khan, whom Shere Dil Khan had intended to seize at an interview, and to blind.

Haji Khan winked to him, by which he understood he was not to come into the tent. Shere Dil Khan, finding he could not maintain himself at Kabul, was about to return to Kandahar. Haji Khan had, no doubt, an understanding with Dost Mohamed Khan, and turned fakir on a sudden. Shere Dil Khan both sent and went to him; but he would not rise from his seat, saying that he had renounced the pomps and vanities of the world; but Dost Mohamed afterwards came to him, and soon persuaded him to accept seventy thousand rupees a-year, or about five thousand pounds sterling, as his minister. He was then made Governor of Bamian; and, having gone out with a large force under the pretence of collecting revenue, he determined to set up for himself. He passed over to Budukshan, and paid a political visit to Murad Beg, of Kunduz; by whom he and his troops were received with marked attention.

He attended Murad Beg—who, by the way, made a successful marauding excursion into Bamian, when I was at Kabul, September 1836, and carried off several hundred people—on his expedition against Fyzabad; and, seeing that the independence he aimed at was not to be attained, he put on the best appearance, and brought back with him to Kabul a great number of envoys from different places in Turkistan. The Ameer, who was his match, received him with open arms, and said that his father was returned, but, the next day, bestowed the government of Bamian on another. About this time one of his servants stole a purse, belonging to the envoy from Murad Beg. Haji Khan sent the thief to the Ameer to be punished; but Dost Mohamed refused to interfere, saying that the guests and the robber were both of his own creating. Subsequently he entered into a treasonable correspondence with Sultan Mohamed Khan, of Peshawur. Dost Mohamed went to take Jelalabad from Ziman Khan. Haji Khan lagged behind at Kabul, and then took leave of Ameen Mohamed Khan, who had been left there as viceroy, and told him that he was going to join Dost Mohamed Khan from Butkhak, which is one march distant from Kabul, on the direct road to Peshawur; but, instead of doing so, he secretly cut through the mountains, joined Sultan Mohamed Khan at Peshawur, and became his naib, or commander-in-chief.

He next commenced a correspondence with the Sikhs; and intended, it is said, to have plundered the treasury of Sultan Mohamed Khan, on its way from Kohat to Bunghush, but was prevented from doing so by having taken the wrong road. He then came with Sultan Mohamed Khan to Jelalabad. They seized the neighbouring villages, and drove out the people; but when the news of a victory gained by Dost Mohamed arrived, they abused the people for leaving their habitations without permission. Haji Khan then came back to Dost Mohamed Khan; who forgave him, saying, "You went to no worse person than my own brother! you did not go to the infidel Sikhs!"

He now, on every Friday, distributes halfpence to the blind. I have more than once seen the poor blind of Kabul feeling their way to his house, in strings of four or five, in the manner recorded in the Scriptures. When he leaves Kabul to join the army, he goes to the Zearat, or tomb of Shah Sheyd, an Afghan martyr, implores a momentary blessing from the saint, and trots off. When the Sikhs and Afghans were fighting at Peshawur, he received information that Runjit Sing was coming, with only four or five regiments of infantry, from Attok to the camp of the main army at Peshawur; and he offered to Dost Mohamed to lead round the whole body of the Afghan cavalry by a route that was little known, cut off Runjit Sing's escort, and bring the ruler of the Punjab back a prisoner by the same way as he had gone. It was generally supposed that he would have succeeded; but Dost Mohamed was suspicious, and refused his offer. Haji Khan still contrived, when I was at Kabul, to be an influential person; but Mr. Masson, who favoured me with the preceding notice, informed me also, that at the same time he would perhaps receive a secret letter from Runjit Sing, inviting him to forsake Dost Mohamed and join the Sikhs. He would then show the letter to Dost Mohamed, and also a magnanimous answer which he will say he is going to send; intending all the while to send one of a different import. Of such stuff, and much worse, are composed the men who usually line the walls of an Oriental Durbar.

Such is the confusion of names and families connected with the modern history of Kabul, that a short notice of previous events, which I have endeavoured to render as clear and succinct as possible, will not, I hope, be found unacceptable; if it be merely to save the trouble of reference to any other work. This reason and the interest of the moment are my apology for writing what has already been written so often and so well.

Turen, say the most learned of the Afghans, had two sons; Panjpay, and Zeeruk. Panjpay, as the name signifies, had five sons, from whom five families are descended; the Alizyes, the Ishakzyes, the Nurzyes, Marku, and Konjani. Zeeruk had three sons, or families; the Populzyes, the Alukzyes, and Barukzyes; of which latter family is Dost Mohamed, the late Ameer, or King, of Kabul; whilst Shah Shuja and Shah Ziman, whom I saw at Lodiana, are Sirdozyes, or descendants of the Populzyes or elder branch of the family. There are now about seven of these principal Zyes, or families, in Afghanistan; the Sirdozyes, the Barukzyes, Alukozyes, Busizyes, Norzyes, Alizyes, and Ishakzyes. Of all these tribes, the Norzyes, between Kandahar and Herat, are the most numerous. The great men of the Barukzyes naturally took up their residence near Dost Mohamed Khan. The Sirdoyzes and a few Barukzyes resided with Shah Kamran, son of Shah Mahmud, a Sirdozye, at Herat. The whole of these Zyes, or families, have been called Duranis since the time of Achmet Shah, the successor of Nadir Shah. Achmet Shah was the first who took the name of Durani; I know not why. Before his time they were called Abdallis. The Duranis are Afghans. The Sirdozyes owe their rise to Achmet Shah; he was with Nadir Shah when he was assassinated, but immediately came to Kandahar, where he built a city called Achmet Shahi. He then made himself master and king of Kabul, and was succeeded by his son, Timour Shah, whose name is still revered in Afghanistan.

Dost Mohamed Khan did not effect his rise to the throne of Kabul without experiencing his full share of those triumphs and reverses which fall to the lot of every Mussulman who possesses himself of power. Of the fifty or sixty sons of Timour Shah the Sirdozye, there were four that figured conspicuously in the history of Kabul; the Shahs Mahmud, Ziman, Shuja, and Ayub. When Timour Shah died, Ziman was governor of Kabul. He seized upon his three-score of brothers, and put them in prison in the Bala Hissar, with the exception of

Mahmud, who was governor of Herat, and Shuja, who was very young, and a brother by the same mother. Mahmud quarrelled with Ziman, assembled an army, fought and took him prisoner, and blinded him, in revenge for a similar barbarity inflicted by Ziman upon Humaoun, own brother of Mahmud. Mahmud enjoyed the throne for six years. At the time Shah Ziman was blinded, Shuja was at Peshawur, but assembled an army to revenge his brother Ziman; and, after six years of desultory warfare and two battles, he besieged and took Kabul, and made Mahmud prisoner, and talked of taking out his eyes, but Ziman, to his honour, dissuaded him from it. Mahmud escaped from confinement in the Bala Hissar, and fled to Tehran. Shah Ziman having killed Poynder or Surfaraz Khan, the first Barukzye nobleman of distinction at Kandahar, and father of Dost Mohamed Khan, Futi Khan, one of the twenty-one sons of Poynder Khan, went to Tehran, brought back Mahmud, and took Kandahar, having passed through Herat, which was in the possession of another brother of Mahmud, Feroz-ud-Dyn. Shah Shuja, then King of Kabul, was at Peshawur; and Kabul was in the hands of Shah's-ada Hyder, son of Shah Ziman, who fled as Mahmud approached the city. Mahmud and Shuja met near the bridge of Gundamuk; and the result, as is well known, was in favour of the former. Afterwards they fought at Peshawur; again, in another year, at Kandahar: the result, in both instances, was unfavourable to Shuja. Seven years afterwards, Mahmud went with his minister, Futi Khan, to Kandahar; and sent him forward to take Herat, having quarrelled with Feroz-ud-Dyn. Young Dost Mohamed Khan, now the ex-Ameer of Kabul, went with the foregoing expedition; and signalized himself, not in action, but in the Zunana of

Feroz-ud-Dyn, which he forcibly entered, and, amongst his other pranks, gave chase to Rokya Begum, daughter of Timour Shah, and sister to Shah Mahmud, pursued her into a bath, where she had taken refuge, tore off by force from her person the Bund-i-pajama, or waist-band of her trousers, which was studded with very valuable pearls, and escaped with his prize to his brother in Kashmir. Futi Khan wrote to Mohamed Azim Khan, telling him to seize Dost Mohamed, and a guard was placed over him, but before any further steps were taken, news arrived that Futi Khan had been blinded by Kamran, son of Mahmud. The insulted Begum sent her dress, torn and bandless, to her cousin Kamran, at Herat, who forthwith followed Futi Khan,—took him prisoner as he returned from Khorassan, where he had been defeated by the Persian Prince, Ali Mirza, and on the principle which considers that what is done by one man, is done by his family, put out Futi Khan's eyes, to avenge the insult offered by Dost Mohamed to his own cousin. It was finally arranged, that Dost Mohamed Khan should march upon Kabul from Kashmir. He was supplied with two thousand horse, and two laks of rupees. He first came to Peshawur, then governed by Shah Ayub. He paid Ayub honour as King of Kabul, and Ayub gave him assistance, on condition that he himself should be made King *de facto,* in case of Dost Mohamed's success; and sent his son with him also. At this time, Mahmud and the Prince Kamran were at Kandahar. Jehan Guire, Kamran's son, had advanced to Kabul with six thousand men. Atar Mohamed Khan, a Durani, of the Bamzye family, neither Barukzye, nor Sirdozye, was the resident governor of Kabul, on behalf of Jehan Guire, and treacherously invited Dost Mohamed to advance. Some skirmishing took place near the city. The faithless friends of Jèhan Guire Mirza advised him to retire into the Bala Hissar, with two thousand horse. Dost Mohamed bribed a baker, to allow a mine to be run under a tower, through his oven; blew up the tower, and so frightened Jehan Guire that he made his escape in the night through the Dewaseh Kashi, or painted gate, a small portal on the south side of the Bala Hissar. He then fled through the Hazara mountains to Herat. Pir Mohamed Khan, a Barukzye, and brother of Dost Mohamed Khan, soon after took out Atar Mohamed Khan's eyes with his own hand. Mohamed Azim Khan then came from Kashmir, leaving Nawab Jubar Khan, brother of Dost Mohamed Khan, governor of Kashmir, whom the Sikhs soon afterwards drove out, when they took the valley. Azim Khan went to Peshawur, brought Ayub with him to Kabul, and wished to make him king, instead of Ayub's brother, Sultan Ali, whom Dost Mohamed, forgetting his promise to Ayub, had placed upon the throne of Kabul. No battle took place, nor bloodshed, excepting that caused by the death of Sultan Ali, who was killed by Ayub, his own brother, previously to his ascending the throne. Sultan Ali occupied the throne for only two months, when Shah Mahmud and Prince Kamran advanced in force from Kandahar, in order to settle the disturbances at Kabul. They had reached the village of Chahah Asyar, or the four mills; when suspecting treachery,—and just as Dost Mohamed Khan, who was Sultan Ali's General, was on the eve of flying with two thousand horse to Kohistan, at the foot of the mountain,—they retired back to Ghuzni. Finding, when too late, that they had been deceived, they then returned to Kandahar; but so exasperated were they with the behaviour of the Barukzye, that when on the march towards Kabul, they ordered Futi Khan, the great enemy of the Sirdozye, their own family, to be brought out and cut to pieces, in the presence of the whole army. Shah Ayub had been on the throne, as a mere puppet, for eight years, and Mohamed Azim Khan had acted as his minister. Dost Mohamed Khan was merely at this time a Sirdar, or officer about the court. Mohamed Azim Khan upon one occasion went to Shikarpore to collect revenue; he had got as far as Ghuzni, when he was obliged to return, in consequence of hearing that Dost Mohamed Khan had rebelled, and set up for king a Sirdozye, Shahsada Munsur, a son of Shah Ziman. This affair was settled amicably, and then Mohamed Azim Khan, and Shah Ayub, returned towards Shikarpore, taking Dost Mohamed with them. Mohamed Azim Khan had told the Scindians, that he must have thirty-five laks; and the money would perhaps have been paid, had not Dost Mohamed formed a plan for plundering the camp; and in consequence of the confusion, Mohamed Azim Khan was obliged to return, contented with only two or three laks.

Mohamed Azim Khan, after retiring from Shikarpore, next undertook an expedition against the Sikhs. He advanced as far as Naushera, about half-way between Peshawur and Attok, when he was told, so I was informed, that Dost Mohamed had made an attack upon his treasure, which, with his harem, he had ordered to remain upon the western side of the Peshawur river. This part of the story may be doubted, as Mr. Moorcroft, who was in the country at the time, makes no mention of it. He immediately retreated, and with the loss of two or three thousand men, chiefly Ghazis, or religious heroes, (so Mussulmen are termed when fighting against the infidels,) who were principally of the Mohmund, and Eusofzye tribes, returned to Kabul, and died of a broken heart. Dost Mohamed Khan, upon the death of Mohamed Azim Khan, went to Shah Ayub, called him his sovereign, and fought for him on the Ghuzni country, but was three times defeated by Abib Ullah, who also put Ayub in prison, and caused his son Shah's-ada Ismael to be shot.

Abib Ullah Khan, son of Mohamed Azim Khan, now at Lahore, next became master of the country. His father, when dying, placed his son's hand in that of the Nawab Jubar Khan, brother of Dost Mohamed Khan, who would most likely have been his friend, but being dissipated and headstrong, he took from the Nawab the government of the Gilzyes, the tribe that inhabits a large tract of country on the left of the road between Kabul and Ghuzni.

He appointed Dost Mohamed to the government of the Kohistan, but contrived to quarrel with him; and Dost Mohamed, with Shere Dil Khan, his brother, (before of Kandahar,) advanced and blockaded Abib Ullah Khan, in Kabul, then invited him out, and made him prisoner. Dost Mohamed thus became master of Kabul, A. D. 1824, but could not, I believe, then retain it. He, however, re-instated his brother, the Nawab, in the government of the Gilzyes; which, nevertheless, he afterwards took from him, charging Shere Dil Khan with treachery towards Abib Ullah Khan, quarrelling and fighting with him for four or five months. It was about this time that Dost Mohamed Khan won over to himself the services of Haji Khan, whose life I have before attempted to sketch, and who was considered as the first soldier in Kabul. The quantum of organization amongst Afghan troops, and the limits of the superintending powers exercised by an Afghan leader, may be estimated by the fact, that latterly, whilst their troops were fighting in a different part of the field, the two leaders, Dost Mohamed Khan and Shere Dil Khan, were positively adjusting their difference over a plate of cherries! But the Patans are like children in their feelings, as easily excited, and as easily pacified. As Orientals, they are a good and a brave people. They are better than the Persians, without their vivacity; and braver than the Kashmirians, without their cunning. Mr. Elphinstone says, that of all the Orientals, the Afghans are the only people who are susceptible of the passion of love, in the European sense of the word. The mind of the Afghan is far better conditioned than that of the Hindu; whom I have known, when condemned to death, ask for an exhibition of dancing-girls, even in the condemned cell, and who will leap with a smile from the scaffold under the gallows, after having been assured that an extra quantity of wood would be heaped on his funeral pyre.

Shere Dil Khan returned to Kandahar, and Sultan Mohamed Khan Barukzye, brother of Dost Mohamed Khan, was left at Kabul. Dost Mohamed held the government of the Kohistan for about a year, but rebelled, and drove his brother out, and became wholly master of Kabul. Soon after, Fur Dil, Khan Ram Dil, and Meer Dil, came to Ghuzni with an army; but were met by Dost Mohamed, and retreated, after an adjustment of their differences.

The ex-Ameer, Dost Mohamed, stands about five feet ten in height, of a spare and sinewy figure. The upper part of his face is handsome; the forehead high, but not prominent; the nose aquiline; eyebrows high and arched; the eyes large, and very expressive. The worst part of his face is the mouth, which is large and coarse. His appearance altogether is very *distingué*. He dresses in better taste than any man in the Durbar, and his address and manners are far superior to those of any other Durani. He usually sat in a small room in the Bala Hissar, which commanded a view of the city, the parade-ground, and the peaks of the Hindu Kosh. The room, as with others in Kabul, is ornamented with rosettes and other figures, stamped upon a composition paste of talc, which has somewhat the elegant appearance of chased silver, and altogether produces a very pleasing effect.

On the first evening of my introduction, the Durbar was fully attended. There might be about fifty-five persons present; amongst them were Duranis and Kuzzelbashes. I was seated next to the Nawab Jubar Khan, with my Anglo-Persian dictionary by my side, when the Ameer entered. Every one stood up to receive him. He immediately turned to me, and the Nawab told me to give him my hand; which he took, repeating his Khosh amdeh aid!—"You are welcome!"—with great emphasis and much apparent sincerity. I presented him with a case of small pistols, with screw barrels. He examined them, snapped one of them out of the window, and asked how far they would carry. I replied, that they would carry much further than any one present would believe. The next day, Mohamed Akber Khan, his second son, who had been trying them, remarked that they were very good, and that he was much pleased with them. We then sat down on the carpet, and he commenced a conversation, asking numerous questions about the different countries I had seen, particularly about the Nya-Duniah,—"New World," or America,—which he heard I had visited, as to its riches, the number of inhabitants, the animals, and many particulars; and said that he thought a traveller's life must be very good fun. We then had a dissertation upon the comparative merits of Turkoman and Arab horses. He questioned me much about our own English breed, displaying throughout very just ideas upon every subject that he treated. At this moment a black-whiskered mullah entered the room, marched up, and sat himself down immediately beside me. There was something about him that taught me at once what his profession was, and why he had come. I was not wrong in my surmises; he commenced by tapping me on the shoulder in order to attract my attention, and, without further preface, began:—"I say, how did Christ get up through the seven heavens, as you say he did ?" and, suiting the action to the word, placed his hands one above the other, by way of representing the ceilings of the different heavens. I regretted very much that my then very imperfect knowledge of Persian prevented me from proceeding with the argument, as I could have wished. I believe I somehow contrived to admit, that it must have been very difficult; and, as the priest got no further answer, he looked round the Durbar in triumph. This was, I believe, the same person whom Lieutenant Burnes puzzled, by asking, how a man could say Mussulman prayers at the North Pole; for which, I understood, he obtained great credit amongst the learned at Kabul; and whom, Mr. Wolfe, when questioned by him, and rather jeeringly, on the nature of the resurrection, silenced by a counter-question on the subject of his own birth. When at a loss in an argument, a Mussulman immediately retreats back upon the Koran; and, when he has uttered the words, "It is written in the book," it may be said to follow generally that the dispute must cease; since to call in question, at such a moment,—although it may be done sometimes,—the validity of the Koran, would be a wide departure from the guarded course which ought to be pursued by a traveller in a Mohamedan country, particularly on the subject of religion.

I observed at once the difference between the courts of Runjit Sing and Dost Mohamed, and the mummeries that were acted before Shah Shuja in his retreat at Lodiana. I thought of the shawl tents of Runjit, and the jewelled magnificence of the Sikhs who surrounded the person of their chief,—not one of them, not even an European officer, was allowed to sit on the ground without permission,—and I compared his Durbar with the one before me. The chief appeared himself, sitting on a carpet in one corner of the room, and every one else sat where and how he liked; simply, upon entering, making his bow, accompanied with the salaam Alaikoum, or "Peace be with you!" and then retiring to place himself wherever he could find an opening amongst the visitors who lined the wall of the room. The only sign of a king being present was that exhibited by a master of ceremonies, who made more noise than any one else, in endeavouring to preserve order and silence. I also thought again of Shah Shuja at Lodiana; the royal recess in which he sat enthroned to receive visitors; the ranks of bare-footed attendants who stood around, with their hands resting on their girdles, in the most approved Oriental fashion; Baron Hugel and myself, with Captain Wade, the political agent,—to whom he must necessarily be obliged for every application to Government on his behalf,—denied even the privilege of sitting on a chair in his presence. I believe that I myself am one of the very few who had then ever received such an honour; and it was granted me at my own request, when I went to take his portrait.

The next in rank to the Ameer Dost Mohamed Khan was the Nawab Jubar Khan, who was generally in the Durbar, with several of his followers. Another brother, Pir Mohamed Khan, brother of Sultan Mohamed Khan, of Peshawur, was not so frequent a visitor. There was another brother in Kabul, who was so ill as to be always confined to his bed. There were also present Haji Khan, commander of the cavalry, whom I have already noticed; and Abdul Samut, a Persian, originally I believe a private in Colonel Skinner's horse, in India; and two other Naybs, or generals, whose names I forget. The language of the Afghans is Poshtu; the Tajiks, or aborigines of the country, speak Poshtu and Persian. In the Durbar there is more Poshtu than Persian spoken, and more Persian than Turki. If Dost Mohamed addresses an Afghan, he speaks Poshtu. To the Kuzzelbash of Kabul, and visitors from Turkistan, he speaks Turki. Persian is spoken occasionally by all. I breakfasted several times with the Ameer in the Durbar, and on two or three occasions sat next to him, when he would help me with his own royal fingers from his own dishes. "I hear," said he, one day, "that the Feringis never eat with their fingers." I told him he had heard aright. "And why is it so?" said he. "The ladies would not allow it." "Why not?" he said. "Because," I replied, but not without some hesitation, "they would say it was not cleanly." "Why not cleanly? I wash my hands always before I eat," showing them to me at the same time. They were certainly as white and clean as hot water alone—for they rarely use soap—could make them. I then had no other answer to give than that it was not the custom. "No! and there is no other reason for it, either," growled out the black-whiskered mullah aforesaid, who had been listening all the time to what had been said.

Mohamed Akber Khan, the second son of Dost Mohamed,—he who was approaching to raise the late siege of Ghuzni, as already noticed,—was a well-meaning, spirited, fat, but handsome, young man, and usually seated near him in Durbar. He was the favourite son by a favourite wife, whose influence kept him in his place. Mohamed Afzul Khan, the eldest son, was absent, collecting tribute during the whole time I was at Kabul. I heard a very good account of him, but he is motherless, and has fewer friends in the Zunana. A promising young scapegrace, named Hyder Khan, now a prisoner at Lodiana, is the next brother. He was learning to govern by residing at Charika, near the Kohistan, or country at the foot of the Hindu Kosh, of Kabul; and had some of his horses stolen one night by the Kohistanis, when Mr. Masson and myself were visiting Beghram. A younger brother of Hyder Khan, Mohamed Ameen Khan, was often resting on his father's knee. Two or three others, mere children, would sometimes make their appearance in Durbar, to get a kiss, or a rupee, from their father and the Nawab.

Nothing could be more simple than the fare of Dost Mohamed Khan. In the morning, about eight or nine o'clock, a number of melons were brought into the Durbar, and were eaten in an unripe state, at least not so much ripened as we should eat them in England. It is frightful to see an Oriental cutting away at an unripe melon, and swallowing every part of it excepting the green outside. Numerous deaths are the consequence of this pernicious practice, and every large town in the East is more or less afflicted by sickness during the melon season. In about an hour after the fruit had been demolished, a more substantial breakfast was brought in. The dishes contained nothing but mutton, over-roasted or boiled to rags, with or without vegetables, and covered with the rice of Peshawur, the finest in the world. Its grains, when boiled, swell out to a length of three-fifths of an inch. Perhaps eight or ten persons would remain behind in the Durbar, to partake of this meal; the others would retire, from inclination rather than etiquette; at least I did not think that invitations to remain and eat were given beforehand. The dinner, or rather supper, was of the same kind, after the evening Durbar. I had once thus an opportunity of seeing Dost Mohamed more *en famille;* he played at chess with one of the chiefs present, and the others merely conversed or watched the game. Dost Mohamed seemed to enjoy it amazingly, although he was, if I rightly recollect, beaten. An extension of the hand to that of his antagonist, accompanied with a hearty squeeze, was the method by which he expressed his delight at having taken a piece from him. A similar action usually attends the understanding a joke, or a play upon words; and when, in the East, the parties happen to be standing near each other, and are old friends, I have seen them bow their heads till their foreheads met, laughing heartily all the time, by way of intimating how much in unison are their feelings upon the subject of their mirth. Whilst the Ameer was playing at chess, I sat down to make a portrait of his son, Mohamed Ameen Khan.

A few prints, which I had with me, were often produced in the Durbar. Two were frequently exhibited by particular desire; one was a portrait of Her Majesty Queen Adelaide. It was a print; but its value, in their ideas, was much enhanced by the colouring which I had purposely added; and flattering and numerous were the encomiums which were universally lavished upon the Taj-i-Dowlah—"Crown of the state"—of England. Another was an excellent mezzotinto of a French lady,—Mademoiselle Mars, I believe; which was seized upon, after having been frequently exhibited, by Mohamed Akber Khan, and search was made, I fear unsuccessfully, throughout Kabul for a piece of glass that was necessary to render its framing complete. My own attempts at portrait-taking were altogether sufficiently successful in the Durbar and elsewhere to elicit the approbation of the Kabul connoisseurs; who, so far from showing anything like an aversion to the art, were constantly requesting me to take their pictures. I used frequently to pass my mornings in the large open rooms of the new building in the Bagh-i-Shah, or "king's gardens." An assembly of some of the first people in Kabul was usually there, and the Prince Mohamed Akber Khan was sometimes there also. His own Mirza, a very good-natured person, but singularly ugly, was committed to paper by me, at the request of the Prince himself. The company were convulsed with laughter; but he peremptorily ordered the man to come and sit down opposite to me. He requested me, in an imploring tone, not to look at him; but, when the likeness was finished, the Prince handed it about with the greatest glee, and indulged in a hearty laugh at the expense of the abashed Mirza, in which he was, of course, joined by every body in the room. At the Prince's own request I made a picture of himself, on horseback, in complete armour. In this I was happy enough to please him, only he wanted a long slip of paper stuck on the top of the picture, in order that he might see the full length of an enormous spear which he held in his hand. "Of what use would that be?" said the Ameer; "any one can see what it is you have in your hand." Dost Mohamed Khan is himself a good critic on animal painting. He is one of the very few Orientals who can comprehend, without a question, the meaning of a shadow, or why one side of the face should be dark and the other light, and why, in some positions, more of one eye should be seen than the other. When an Oriental is presented with a picture, he usually turns it upside down, unless its subject be very obvious

MAHOMED AKBER KHAN,

Favorite Son of Dost Mohamed Khan, and Commander of his Cavalry

London. Published by Whittaker & C[o] Ave Maria Lane.

indeed. I drew some of the Ameer's favourite horses. He seldom flattered, often found fault, but always in good taste. He liked evidently to see a horse pourtrayed with all its faults, where they existed; not desiring that either the crest should be raised, or the quarters enlarged, according to the fancy of the painter, as is always the case in the East. Dost Mohamed is as fond of horses as his powerful rival, Runjit. In the hot weather he rode every day, attended by some of his courtiers, to the Bagh, or garden of Timour Shah, where he used to sit, on a raised and carpetted platform, sheltered from the heat by a wooden roof, and the shade of aspen and mulberry trees; whilst before and around him were picketted, perhaps, three hundred horses; his favourites, of course, being quite close to him. The nearest was a very fine iron-grey, three year old, a son of his celebrated horse "Tawus," or the "peacock," which had been sent, I believe, as a present to Bahadür Khan, the Ameer of Bokhara. The horses of Afghanistan are not so coarse as the Turkoman horses, but are fine, powerful, and spirited animals, with good heads, and deep in the carcase; but there were none of them that would bare competition with our own English thorough-bred. The quarter is too much flattened, the tail set on too low, the joints lengthened, and the best of them had nothing of the long, firm, and elastic stride of our race-horse. I told him, that although his cattle were as good as the country afforded, yet that they were nothing in comparison with our own: he believed me, and looked envious, but certainly not angry, and inquired more about them, their speed, and their prices.

The Turkoman horse is a large, loosely made, and bony animal, usually with a very coarse head, and badly put on; and sometimes a long ill-shaped eye: his stamina is surprising. Wonderful are the stories related of his performances, and though I will never believe that the horse of a Turkoman, or any other horse in the world, can equal that of an English thorough-bred; nevertheless, I consider, that a cross between the Turkoman and the English blood would produce the very best description of hunter. A well-bred Turkoman horse could easily be sent from Persia to England, *viâ* Trebizonde.

The last portrait I attempted was that of the Ameer Dost Mohamed Khan himself; no one could possibly sit quieter. I was not at first quite satisfied with my own performance, and my alarms about a failure were not dissipated by the remarks of the flatterers in the Durbar, who usually said it was not like, and never could be. The

Ameer's Mullah, my black-whiskered disputant, was my aversion, which I was at no pains to conceal, at least as far as grimace went; although the Ameer, observing my distress, assured me one day that he was a very good man. Being a holy person, he claimed the privilege of thumbing my drawings, and running his fingers over the pencil-marks, which I never allowed any one else to do. The Ameer himself came and sat by me whilst I was taking his picture, and nothing could be more gentleman-like than his remarks, which were so much in contrast with those made by others. At my request, he pointed out the parts which he thought like and unlike, adding that he might be wrong, as he did not sufficiently know his own features. One day a stout, little, rosy-cheeked boy, toddled up to his father, in full durbar: he had evidently been sent in by his mother, to be admired and drawn; and the

Ameer asked me to take his picture. I replied, which was the truth, that I had not then time : he either did not hear, or misunderstood me, exclaiming, with a loud laugh, in which his oriental ideas of etiquette could not restrain him from indulging, "The Sahib says, he is not handsome enough," and was clearly chuckling at the idea of how angry the child's mother would be, when he told her what I had just said.

By the Nawab's protection, and the Ameer's permission, I was enabled to go about sketching every where, and was for twenty-one days in succession posted on the hill of Asha-Mahi, "Mother Eve," in view of the whole city of Kabul, finishing a panoramic drawing, which many, no doubt, would have prevented if they could. One man only, a Syud, or descendant of the Prophet, went to the Ameer, and asked him to forbid me, saying that I could look down into his Zunana: "Nonsense," said the Ameer; "what can he see at that distance above you?" and forthwith dismissed his complaint. The Nawab also spoke to him, and I forthwith sent the man my salaam, and a small present, so that he afterwards, as did many others, paid me a visit on the hill. One day while sketching the entrance to the bazaar, a fanatic mullah, who had come in from the country, observing me in the act of drawing, immediately concluded, that I was going to take bodily possession of the whole country, and shouted out that he would call all the mullahs, and raise the city against me. The good Nawab had always appointed one of his wrestlers to attend upon me; he and some others instantly went down and spoke to the man, and quieted him, by informing him that I was under the Nawab's protection. Such was the liberal treatment I met with in this Mussulman country, and at a time too, when the Afghans were annoyed, because their complaints against the Sikhs had not been attended to, and their letters requesting the interference of the Indian government had remained unanswered.

In estimating the character of Dost Mohamed Khan, we find him entitled to a considerable share of that lenity, which makes allowance for the want of education. With similar lenity the past character of such a person should be viewed as affecting the consideration of the present. He is a reformed man: when young he played, as I have already mentioned, the assassin: having heard that his brother, Futi-Khan, had expressed his dislike to some person, and shortly after meeting that person in the bazaar, he took him round the waist, and stabbed him, but was forgiven on account of his youth. When he was king, he entirely abandoned the use of wine, and conformed in all respects to the dicta of the Koran, at least so much so as to satisfy the Mullahs; the strictest penalties were inflicted upon those who drank wine, and wine-vessels were broken wherever they were found, excepting in the houses of the Armenians, who, being Christians, were exempted from search. There were several Armenian families in Kabul.

With regard to the morals of Kabul, there are few places where they are at a lower ebb; and the attempts to restrain immorality by penalties, were alike iron-handed, incongruous, and productive of evil. There were no singing or dancing girls allowed; and whilst the frailties of the sex were visited with the utmost severity, the other remaining vices of the catalogue were allowed to run riot, without stigma, repression, or even discouragement. Although, perhaps, the sincerity of the Ameer's religious opinions might be doubted, there can be no doubt that he was aware of the advantage of putting on the semblance of piety. What ruler is not? He had several Mullahs in his train, who directed him in matters connected with the faith, and at the same time were made use of, to conciliate their turbulent brethren in the city, who, ever ready for a change, would come forth, arrayed in winding-sheets, and proclaim a religious war upon very little provocation, and terrify even the firm nerves of the Ameer.

The Nawab Jubar Khan can neither read nor write: while as a proof of the superior mind of the Ameer, and of his energetic determination, he had taken the trouble to learn to read at the age of forty-five or fifty.

Kabul was distracted by parties, that were not unwilling to dethrone him, but could not agree as to whom they should place upon the musnud. But it was easy to see that all the rest were mere fools to him, in point of talent; and I have not been mistaken, in supposing that he would keep his place, in spite of all internal dissension. It appeared to me surprising, that they should wish to displace him. In the time of Shah Shuja, a man could hardly go ten or fifteen miles from the city, without imminent risk of being robbed, and perhaps murdered. The more determined administration of Dost Mohamed Khan had made the roads safe for a much greater distance. He seized and executed several of the most powerful leaders of the refractory tribes, who inhabit the mountains of Nejrou, Taghou, and the Kohistan of Kabul: he had a good understanding with Saadut

Khan, the chief of the powerful Mohmund Afghans; and, on the other hand, his name was beginning to be respected amongst the wild tribes who inhabit the mountainous frontiers beyond Ghuzni. His revenue, since the loss of Kashmir, Peshawur, and the provinces to the west of the Indus (Attok or Sinde), did not exceed twenty-three laks, which in Kabul rupees, averaging about two-thirds of the value of those of Hindustan, is equivalent to about 160,000*l*. sterling. The poorness of his treasury kept his invention for ever on the stretch; and I heard, that many an act of injustice had been committed, for the sake of procuring money. Property was sometimes seized, and lists were made out of those who were able to spare a little, but who generally preferred paying, to going to prison. His excuse for all this was, that without it government could not be carried on; and yet if any one else had held the reins in Kabul, matters would have been ten times worse. The chief himself, having run his career through adventure of every complexion, was well acquainted with the character of his countrymen, and was naturally suspicious of all around him: being alike unassisted and unimpeded by laws, his motives for surveillance were doubly imperative, and the vigorous measures which he felt himself obliged to adopt were, no doubt, often and unjustly tinged with the imputation of tyranny. He took care to keep up at least the semblance of justice towards the lower classes of his subjects, and I have before remarked, that it was a common saying amongst them, "Is Dost Mohamed dead, that there is no justice?" A soldier demanded his discharge when the treasury was empty, because he could not get his pay. The Ameer said, that it should never be told, that Dost Mohamed Khan has refused a man payment of his just demand, and gave him his pay, but discharged him from his service. A woman who was missing, was supposed to have been murdered for the sake of her jewels. The suspected murderer was kept in prison for a year, and, being unable to clear himself of the charge, was sentenced to death. I saw him hanging by the feet, after having been impaled on a lofty gallows, erected like that of Haman, opposite to the King's gate. A horrible murder was committed whilst I was at Kabul: blood was observed to drop from a bag, which an old woman was carrying through the bazaar: she said that it contained leeches freshly applied: it was, however, opened in the crowd; and the head of a young and beautiful woman was found in it, with her bridal ornaments upon her brow; to obtain which, she had been sent to sleep by the use of narcotics, and then murdered.

The reign of Timour Shah was still remembered by the older inhabitants of Kabul, as that in which the city enjoyed its greatest modern prosperity. He was a liberally-minded ruler, and was known to lend a man money, and tell him to go and trade with it. The revenue of Dost Mohamed was certainly on the increase; he had overturned the old system of collecting, and generally took one-third of the produce of all lands under cultivation. Yet on a sudden emergency, I have known him exact five or ten rupees from every shop in the bazaar. But the whole of his fiscal revenue did not amount to more than three laks, or about 20,000*l.* sterling. Nothing came into the city without payment of a few pice, or halfpence; every sheep paid one, and one sheep in every forty was the property of the Ameer; an officer, acting as a broker, again taxed them in the market; another duty was paid for the mark which showed that the broker's tax had been paid. The posteen, a leathern jacket maker, or currier, paid half a shahi—about three farthings—in the rupee, according to the value of the posteen; so that the purchaser of the sheep in the market had to pay two or three rupees for it.

When I was in Kabul, Dost Mohamed Khan was in possession of sixty guns, of different calibre; and could at any time command a force of twelve thousand cavalry. The number of irregular infantry depended upon the state of his finances; but it might have been increased, I believe, to eighty or one hundred thousand men, in case of a religious war. The Patans, as horsemen, are more formidable than the Sikhs. Dost Mohamed's disciplined infantry—if such a term may be used when speaking of it—were in a wretched condition, from insubordination and want of accoutrement. I forget their numerical force, but it did not amount to more than a few hundreds.

I several times met Mirza Abdul Sami Khan, the prime-minister. He was a fat, fresh-coloured, and good-natured man, slightly marked with the small-pox, a bon-vivant, and very dissipated. He was the only person in the confidence of the Ameer. In his convivial hours he was generally the merriest of the party, and he always treated me with the most cordial civility. It was amusing, upon state occasions, such as at the introduction of Allahdad Khan, the Tak Rajah, to see him standing at the door with a wand of office, he being one of the greatest men in Kabul; whilst any person of low rank would seat himself without ceremony, after having made his salaam to the Ameer. I was told that he considered himself as a servant. One evening he sent an invitation to supper to Mr. Masson and myself. I was about to leave Kabul shortly afterwards, and the Ameer was exceedingly anxious for the long-delayed answers to the letters which he had sent to the Indian Government. We found but a few guests, and two of the principal singers in Kabul. They sang a great deal; and our host and his guests were apparently much delighted with their performances. He made his remarks to us from time to time, and translated the words. The Afghans had then also, as was well-known, sent to Mohamed Shah of Persia, for assistance against the Sikhs. I had repeatedly told them, that I was in no wise connected with the Government; but no Oriental can understand why a man should travel without having some political reason for so doing. My friend the Nawab and his dependents, when visiting me, were constantly inventing wars and rumours of wars, chiefly from the side of Persia, in order to see what I could say in answer to them: that the Shah was fast approaching Herat, with an immense army; that "Ingeil Sahib," for so they then called Sir John M[c] Neill, had offered them two crore of rupees (two million sterling!) if they would not advance; and fifty other stories equally ridiculous, some of which I laughed at, in order to show that I was not to be deceived in that way, whilst I refuted others by a simple reference to probabilities. The kind Nawab would sometimes taunt me, but good-naturedly, with the change of feeling towards the Afghans, by referring to the golden times of Mr. Elphinstone's mission to Shah Shuja. "Sahib!" said he, "all the good name the English have in these countries is owing to Elphinstone Sahib!" But this was before Sir Alexander Burnes' second mission, as that gentleman's name is revered in every country that he passed through; and no one that ever had only the honour of a word from him failed, as it seemed to me, to call and inquire after him. One man, who showed me a watch he had given him, wished me to take him back to England, that he might again see his master. At this supper, it appears that the minister—most likely by the orders of his master—had determined to try the old game with me. One of his first remarks, for instance, contained a hint to me of the possibility of my being plundered on my return to Hindustan, if the answer to the Governor-General's letter did not arrive in time, or if the contents should not be satisfactory. "You are aware," said he, with a very knowing look, and drawing at the same time a map on the floor with his hands, "that you have a range of mountains to pass between this and Jelalabad, that then you have a plain to cross, and that again, on the other side, you will find the Mohmund Afghans." Confident, however, in the Nawab's protection, and feeling quite sure that at this juncture they would not dare to connive at the robbery of an Englishman, I replied merely by a low bow and a smile. He then proceeded to make remarks of a political tendency upon the wording of the songs, scarcely a syllable of which I could distinguish. Not so Mr. Masson, who, understanding all he sang, was giving me a very significant glance from time to time. He afterwards explained to me the meaning of the songs. The singer was a perfect Davide, in his way, and exhibited a power of execution far superior to any thing I have ever heard in the East. "If he continue to improve as hitherto," remarked the minister, "he will be quite a prodigy. Do you not hear what he sings? 'If we don't get an answer from one city, we will from another! My heart is filled with affliction, and how long are my hopes to be delayed?' It is surprising," he added, "how soon they learn any thing from my teaching. When they go out elsewhere, they sing the songs of Hafiz; but, when they come to my house, they find other themes for their songs." There could be no doubt whatever that he had composed the words himself, by way of eliciting from us some remark on the intentions of the Indian Government towards Kabul.

KAFFIR SLAVES AT KABUL, p. 236.

CHAPTER XII.

Eating the Hulym—Shah Shuja's Expedition and Defeat—Remarks upon the Affairs of Persia, Afghanistan, and the British Policy—Dost Mohamed and his Future Conduct—Khiva—Russian Expedition—Remarks on the Kirghiz Kazaks and their Country—Different Routes to Khiva—Horse-Racing—Anecdote— Commerce of the Kirghiz Kazaks—Mode of Attack of the Kirghiz Kazaks, and Object—Conclusion.

On the twelfth of October, the Ameer and all the grandees of Kabul assembled in the

Nawab's bath, a large, but dark room, heated by flues, to eat the Hulym, a customary dish at the commencement of the cold weather. It is eaten by the Mussulmen in India, as well as in Afghanistan. Mutton and wheat are beaten up together till they form a thick paste; huge dishes, such as are seen in every English dairy, are piled with this composition; a quantity of milled grease and sugar are then added, and it is set before the guests. I was indulged with a spoon; the Ameer and the rest of the company ate with their fingers. Dost Mohamed was certainly a little out of humour, pretended to be much more so, and asked me, in a manner that was somewhat authoritative, to show him my panoramic view of Kabul; which I did, and should have been in some little alarm about it, had I not felt that the Nawab, whose guest I was, and who had before assured me that not a hair of my head should be touched, or any thing in my possession abstracted from me during my stay at Kabul, would have been true to his word. The Ameer inspected half the drawings, and then put them from him, in a pretended huff. He afterwards assumed his usual tone of cordiality; and complained to the Nawab, that I, his guest, did not seem to enjoy the Hulym. I made the best excuse I could for eating but scantily of any thing so very cloying. The Ameer's manner arose entirely out of his anxiety to get an answer from the Indian Government. The good Nawab himself, at parting with me the next morning, put on, for the same reason, an air of coldness and reproach, which he had never till that moment assumed. The long-expected answer arrived but a few days afterwards, and gave, by its contents, universal satisfaction. It is, I believe, the letter contained in the "Correspondence relative to Afghanistan," before Parliament, page 396. One of the chief reasons for the delay upon this occasion, was caused by the interregnum which occurred between the retirement of Lord William Bentinck and the arrival of Lord Auckland.

I have never doubted for an instant the correctness of that line of policy which it *eventually* became necessary to pursue, by sending the late expedition to Afghanistan. I have never doubted for an instant that it would succeed, or that Shah Shuja would be well received by the Afghans. When, at the battle near Kandahar, which he fought with Dost Mohamed in 1834, he ordered his elephant to be turned round, and fled, there were few of the leading men of Kabul who had not commenced an intrigue with him. The Nawab himself asked permission to be allowed to go and make terms with Shah Shuja; but was told by the Ameer, who was suspicious of him, that there would be time enough for that when his own party were beaten.

Mr. Campbell, a gentleman whom I saw at Kabul, in the service of Dost Mohamed, favoured me with the following account of Shah Shuja's unsuccessful expedition from Lodiana, for the recovery of his throne, in 1833-4. He was with Shah Shuja when he left Lodiana, at the end of 1833; and, when first employed, had obtained a company and a gun, and was sent ahead to Malai Koteler. Afterwards, the Shah gave Mr. C. three hundred men and two guns. He had then, altogether, about six or seven hundred men under his command. The guns were bought of the Rani of Tenassee, for one thousand rupees (one hundred pounds). Shah Shuja was encamped at Lodiana for a month, and then went to Malai Koteler, where he remained another month, receiving presents after the Ede. On that day, the Nawab of Malai Koteler gave him five thousand rupees and two horses. Shah Shuja then moved, in three days, to Tigrana. Futi Sing, of Kopatella, next sent him two thousand rupees and some swords; and, in a fortnight afterwards, he went to Bawhulpore, receiving five thousand rupees, a gun, some camels, and bullocks, from the Nawab; thence he marched to Shikarpore. The Vakil of Hydrabad, Kosseyn Shah, went to Kampore, three kos (six miles), to meet Shah Shuja, presented him with fifty thousand rupees and five or six horses, some swords, and two tents, and brought him to Shikarpore, where he remained ten months. In the ninth month he sent a present of a Persian horse, and some tents, to Runjit Sing; who sent him back a lack of rupees in cash. The Ameer of Hydrabad, afterwards getting jealous of Shah Shuja, attacked him, twenty miles from Shikarpore. Shah Shuja beat him, and took four guns; many of the chiefs of Sinde were killed, and Kosseyn Shah was amongst the number. Shah Shuja, in the end, gave the Sindians three lacks out of the five they demanded, and left Shikarpore. He then encamped at a village three miles from Shikarpore; and afterwards marched through the desert the whole night, and arrived at Kundah, a village with a stream. From Shahlmerstan he sent letters to the Ameer of Kelat, desiring him to send him five lacks of rupees, ten horses, and some camels. The Ameer sent him a lack, twenty camels, and three horses, and one horse to Mr. Campbell. Bahadur Khan Kakur, of Sulkhaneh, near Hydrabad, came to Shah Shuja with a lack of rupees, twenty camels, and five horses, and accompanied him to Kandahar at night. He remained in the old town built by Nadir Shah for two months, with sixty thousand men. Afterwards, Dost Mohamed went to Kandahar to oppose him, with twenty thousand horse, five thousand foot, and about eighteen guns. When Dost Mohamed was within twelve miles of the city, Shah Shuja withdrew his guns from the batteries, left the old town, and encamped at Ava Sava. On the following morning Dost Mohamed arrived at Kandahar; on the next, Dost Mohamed's son, Mohamed Akber Khan, came out to fight, with about twelve thousand men, chiefly cavalry I believe, and four guns. There was a battle, without any important result, till, about five o'clock, Shah Shuja ordered Mr. Campbell to go against the enemy, with the two battalions and four guns. The forces were drawn out, but not engaged. One of Shah Shuja's guns burst, and Mr. Campbell was ordered to return to the lines for the evening. Early in the morning Dost Mohamed drew out his forces, in order to give battle. Shah Shuja moved also, but too hastily, and ordered Samunder Khan and Jehan Dad Khan to advance with twelve thousand horse. The rest of the force was ordered to follow; and Mr. Campbell was sent forward with two battalions, but with no guns or cavalry to support him, although he asked for them. Mr. C. informed me, that Shah Shuja, from his elephant, ordered him to "chupao," or rush forward in the native manner. Mr. C. remonstrated, and said he could do more by steady fighting, without breaking his ranks. Shah Shuja, however, was headstrong, and repeated hastily the words, "Chupao! chupao!" and before Mr. C. could again speak to him, he became panic-struck, ordered his elephant to be turned, and fled. Mr. C., however, was engaged for two hours or more; but, being unsupported, he was beaten back. Three hundred Hindustanis, who had been in the

Company's service, sustained the fight for a long time, until they were overpowered by numbers. Mr. Campbell was wounded, and his company obliged to retreat, with the loss of eighty-six men. Whilst lying on the field he was recognized by a mounted soldier of Dost Mohamed, who lifted him up behind him, and galloped off with him. The soldier's name was Mir Akber; he was a servant of Mir Dil Khan, of Kandahar. He washed Mr. C.'s wounds, and took him to his own house. After a week, Dost Mohamed Khan called on Mir Dil Khan, accompanied by the Nawab Jabar Khan, and Mirza Abdul Sami Khan, the minister. They visited Mr. C., and Dost Mohamed called him his son, and assured him that he would be kind to him, and sent him to Kabul on an elephant; where he gave him the command of some guns, and four hundred rupees a-month.

The raising of the siege of Herat has entirely changed the aspect of affairs in the East; and the gallantry, skill, and determination, of Lieutenant Pottinger,—who chiefly conducted its defence,—has saved the British empire in India from consequences, the extent of which cannot be contemplated, but of which enough could be foreseen to enable us to pronounce on the possibility of their seriously, for a time, affecting its very existence. England has now the vantage-ground; and, if she hold her own, and a tight hand be kept over those unfortunate differences of opinion, by which the diplomats, under the meridian of the Indus, are so notoriously agitated, she may snap her fingers at Russia, and have nothing to fear—at least I think not—on the score of successful invasion, whatever may be attempted.

Not to have taken possession of Herat,

after the Persians had retired, is, in my humble judgment, as sound policy, as it would have been to have marched there, supposing the siege had been continued. But afterwards it was right to leave well alone. Between the British dominions in India, and the confines of the Russian dominions, there are three distinct nations, who are enemies to each other by blood, and by religion. The Persians, who are Shiah Mahometans, and very bigoted, are ever ready to quarrel with the Afghans, who are Sunis; and the Sikhs, who are Hindus, can always be let loose upon these last also. Badly conducted indeed must be the diplomacy that could not prevent all, any, or either of them, unassisted by Russia, from doing harm to the British interests in India. When the siege of Herat was raised, the Russians were driven out of the field—to have marched forward in order to take Herat, would have been fretting the Persians to no good purpose, and would have been unjust to Prince Kamran, who, after all, had been fighting our battles for us, and whose hatred to the Persians was only just equalled by his aversion to the Barukzyes, or family of Dost Mohamed Khan. His distrust of us in the first instance could only have been owing to his suspicion, (and who that knows the character of an oriental could doubt it,) and the idea he entertained, that we were going to put his uncle, Shah Shuja, in possession of Herat. He has been undeceived in this particular, and now cannot, I should think, but meet the views of the British Government, in re-establishing the Sirdozyes on the throne of Afghanistan.

The dashing and unexpected manner in which Ghuzni was taken, completely neutralized the whole of the arrangements made by Dost Mohamed Khan for its defence, and secured an easy and successful termination to the campaign. The moral effect that this brilliant exploit, to say nothing of the capture of Kelat, must have produced on the minds of the Asiatics, is as great, perhaps greater, and certainly more extensive, than that of any former British victory in the East. I would say with the greatest deference, that the fame of Plassy and Assaye was local in comparison. From Hydrabad to Bokhara and Kokan, they first learnt that Herat, defended by one British officer, resisted and beat off the Shah of Persia and his thousands; and afterwards were taught to believe, that a handful of British troops after a fatiguing march, halted before the gate of Ghuzni, and forthwith captured their favourite and impregnable fortress in a couple of hours. No piece of service could possibly have been pointed out so likely to extend the reputation of our arms in the East, or so calculated to overawe the insolent, conciliate the disaffected, and awaken a proper and universal respect for the British name, as the taking of Ghuzni in the manner it was accomplished.

But when I say that I might approve of the plan for reinstating Shah Shuja, I wish I could as easily persuade myself, that Dost Mohamed Khan had not been treated with injustice.. It must be remembered, that he twice won his throne by his sword: at first when he established himself, in 1824, and subsequently, when ten years having elapsed, he defeated Shah Shuja, at Kandahar, after which he took the title of "Ameer." I have had, of course, no access to the letters which have passed between him and the British government at an earlier period; but putting together all I have heard, and all I have seen, I have no doubt that, during the whole time which has elapsed since he first made himself master of Kabul, up to the date of his reception of the Russian envoy, both he and his brothers have been most anxious to acquire the friendship and alliance of the East India Company, and sent to Russia and Persia for assistance, only when he was beginning to despair of our taking him by the hand.

Mr. Moorcroft, who was in the country when Dost Mohamed Khan made himself master of Kabul, mentions, (vide Moorcroft's travels, by Wilson, p. 340,) that "at "a former interview, we were most earnestly entreated to become the channel of a "negotiation, for placing the whole country under British rule. So urgent, and "apparently sincere were their representations, that I was obliged to acquiesce so "far as to promise to forward a memorial "from them to Calcutta, stating distinctly, "that it was to be considered as the mere "act of a private individual, without any "authority to advocate their cause, and "without any means of offering even a "conjecture as to the result of the appli- "cation."

I have already mentioned the anxiety that prevailed at Kabul when I was there, because no answers to their letters had arrived, and that an answer did arrive a few days after I left Kabul, and gave great general satisfaction. (Vide Correspondence relating to Persia and Afghanistan, p. 396.) Dost Mahomed was to be held in play till Runjit Sing's death, but was too clever a fellow to be deceived in that way. He had maintained himself in his position in spite of every internal dissension, but was still afraid of the Sikhs, because he could not understand our professions of friendship, without more active interference in his behalf. He used to say, " You wish for a trading treaty; of what use is that to me? you can trade now as much as you like!" The Nawab has more than once remarked to me, "Why do not your countrymen form a Chauni (a cantonment) here? we wish it, why do you delay?" The reason we delayed was, that we could not break through the spirit and meaning of that ill-advised treaty, the execution of which Runjit contrived to obtain from Lord William Bentinck, at the meeting between them at Rupur, in October, 1831, whereby he virtually secured to himself a promise of non-interference with any thing he might do on the west side of the Sutlij. The question may be argued for hours, but will always be found referrible to this event. I am humbly disposed to think, that the value of his alliance has been much overrated; I mean, that it has never been of such moment, that it should be allowed to preclude us from forming another on the further side of his dominions. He might have been sent away just as well satisfied without the paper in question, and would not have dared to detain Peshawur against the wishes of the Indian government.

I would never advocate the formation of perpetual friendship with any native power whatever. The existence of an Hindu power between us and Afghanistan is undoubtedly attended with many advantages; but the consequences of this perpetual friendship with Runjit Sing have been, that although he has kept himself quiet in the plains, his Sirdars and Chiefs in the mountains north of the Punjab (who ought, I think, now to be displaced, in favour of the old and rightful Rajahs,) were become so independent of his rule, that they might with justice have been treated totally as a separate power. An Englishman, even a servant of the Company, could not travel in this country without great risk of insult and detention; and the authority of Runjit, as I once took the liberty of telling him, was as nothing beyond the foot of the mountains.

When I first entered the territories of Gulab Sing, of Jumu, the most powerful of his Rajahs, in 1834, I was detained a whole day in the rain by one of his minions, who refused to furnish me with the porters necessary for the prosecution of my journey to Kashmir, under the pretence that I must allow my baggage to be inspected; although I had with me a guard of twelve Sikh Sepahis, and a Chobdar, or officer of Runjit, bearing a silver mace, and who was ordered by his master to attend upon me, protect me from insult, and supply me with every thing.

I was also, as I have already mentioned, shamefully insulted at Leh, in Ladak, in my way to the source of the western branch of the Indus, by order of the same person; although Runjit, who knew where I wished to go, in full durbar, and in my hearing, had ordered him to give me protection and assistance.

In the beginning of 1835, Runjit had made preparations for the invasion of Sinde: his perpetual friendship with us was of little use; he was told that the promise confined the Company to a non-interference on the west side of the Sutlij, and did not extend to that of the Indus.

Runjit Sing obtained the promise of Rupur, in 1831; in 1835, he took Peshawur, not by force, but by a ruse, whilst an amicable treaty was on the tapis,—Hinc illæ lacrymæ. It was the loss of Peshawur that galled and frightened the Patans. Runjit Sing sent to ask permission for his son, Khuruk Sing, to see the town unmolested by the Patans, who were encamped outside. A strong guard was necessary for his Highness; it advanced through the streets at double-quick time, cleared them of the astonished inhabitants, and the Sikhs have ever since kept possession of the pl ace. Mr. Masson informed me, that he was standing on the roof of a house at the time, in company with Abdul Ghias Khan, a nephew of Dost Mohamed, who was then going, I believe, to Lodiana, to be educated. It signified little to Runjit, that the Fakir Aziz-ud-dyn, his old and faithful secretary, was sitting in conference with Dost Mohamed, at the time the panic spread with the news to the Afghan camp—Dost Mohamed seized one hand, and the Nawab seized the other, and led off the astonished

Fakir between them to his elephant, which was hurried along by the crowd. "Tell it not in Gath," said the old man, I forget the Hindustani, when he returned, "but I was terribly frightened!"

It was at this time, when the troops were approaching each other, that Dost Mohamed offered up this extraordinary prayer —"Allah! I am but as a fly, and am going against an elephant, yet if it be thy will, thou canst make the fly to prevail."

Since then we could not interfere with Runjit, was Dost Mohamed to be blamed for seeking assistance elsewhere, after having sought ours for the preceding ten years? We refused to help him, because we could not break through our agreement with Runjit, and thereby appear to show him, that Afghanistan is not of so much consequence to us as he would imagine. When, however, it became necessary on every account to interfere at Kabul—we entertain a different opinion, and Runjit's consent and co-operation is sought for, and secured by the mission and abilities of Mr. (now Sir William) Mc Naughten, on the 30th May, 1838. Runjit might have been flattered by the humiliation of his old rival, Dost Mohamed, but did not relish the idea of entering into a treaty that would put it out of his power to march to Kabul when he pleased, and render the Rupur paper of little use to him, and one morning, without ceremony, he took himself off to Lahore from Dynanagur, where he received the mission.

We did not assist Shah Shuja when he went from Lodiana, in 1834, which would show at least that we had some respect for Dost Mohamed; but we are in the end, in consequence of our own faulty diplomacy, obliged to turn him off the throne of Kabul, in order to make room for Shah Shuja, and, in so doing, annul the promise given to Runjit, by which we had been so long hampered, and on which he had so long relied.

Runjit Sing, on a late occasion, asked of an Afghan present in his durbar, who was well acquainted with the events that had taken place in Afghanistan during the last half century, whether Dost Mohamed Khan would soon be reconciled to the loss of his kingdom. The answer he received was, that he was a clever fellow, who, after having been beaten, had always been remarkable for coming on again and again, without having had any calculable mode of procuring resources. If Shah Shuja never gave up the idea of restoration to his throne, most assuredly Dost Mohamed Khan will follow his example; hopeless as the idea may be. The last accounts say that he has taken refuge in Turkistan. There was no other course for him to pursue, excepting that of surrender to the British. Had he retreated towards Persia, Shah Kamran, at Herat, would probably have taken out his eyes, or perhaps have put him to death. He may still, perhaps, calculate upon assistance from Persia; and if the Russians take Khiva, he will commence an intrigue with them forthwith: they will receive his information and his overtures with caution, and can offer none but conditional promises, but will always find him a ready listener to any proposals of a political nature, which they may think it worth their while to make.

It is superfluous to remark, that Burnes, Conolly, and Stirling, from their own travels and personal experience, have given us very able notices of Central Asia, and the regions lying to the north of the Hindu Kosh. Khiva, amongst the orientals south of that range, is generallly known by the name of its principal city Hurghunge, *i. e.* Houri-Gunge (signifying, the town or place, I believe, of the Houris): it was so named, I think, by Timour Lung (Tamerlane), either from the beauty of the place, or of the women; and the Great Desert (Sahara), or plain of Central Asia, is usually called by them the Dusht, or plain of Kuptchak. M. Moravief, in his voyage in Turkomania, describes the country of Khiva as a rich oasis watered by irrigation from the Amu, or Oxus, on which it is situated, and highly productive. He estimates its length and width at more than one hundred miles; says that it contains five considerable towns and many villages, and that three hundred thousand persons acknowledge the Khan of Khiva as their sovereign. From its centre to the banks of the Caspian, extends a vast and arid steppe, three hundred miles in extent, which is passed by camels in seventeen days. On the north it is bounded by the course of the Amu, or Oxus, that empties itself into the sea of Aral; on the south-east a steppe separates it from the kingdom of Bokhara, and on the south-west it is separated by sandy plains and steppes from Teke, which he adds is an oasis refreshed by water-courses swollen by the rain. The latitude of the town of Khiva is forty-one degrees, forty minutes; and its longitude, from the Island of Ferro, seventy-eight degrees, ten minutes.

A person to whom I applied for information at Kabul, informed me that from Bokhara to Hurghunge, it was a nine days' march, Moravief says seven, with camels, and five with horses; but that the route could only be traversed for three months in the year, when water could be procured from melting the snow. From Hurghunge to Orenburg it was twenty-three days with camels, and ten days with horses; and that this road also could only be passed in the spring. The great Kirghiz lake, or sea ot Aral, was reached in four days by camels. By the other route, direct from Bokhara to Jaman-Kala, Yemen-Killah, or Orsk, on the frontiers of Russia, it was a thirty days' march for camels, and twenty for horses. The first Russian mission to Khiva was sent by Peter the Great, but the unfortunate Prince Bekevitch, who commanded it, was cruelly assassinated.

In 1813 another attempt was made to open a negotiation with the Turkomans, who forthwith sent ambassadors to request the assistance of Russia against the Persians. But as they arrived at a time when the Russians were concluding a friendly treaty with the Persians, the Turkomans were obliged to retire in disgust.

M. Moravief was dispatched in 1819: the object of his mission, as declared in his conversation with the Khan of Khiva, appears to have been simply to induce the Khan to order his trading caravans to come directly to the port of Krasnorodsk, on the Caspian, and there dispose of their merchandise, after a march which would occupy only seventeen days; instead of allowing them to proceed as usual, by the old route to Monghichlak, which was without water, and occupied a month. The Khan replied, that the tribes on the route to Monghichlak were devoted and submissive to him, whereas on the proposed route the caravans would certainly be pillaged by the Kadjurs (Persians), and that therefore he could not consent to such an arrangement. It does not appear, whether any new arrangement was made in consequence of this mission.

Part of the instructions from the Russian head-quarters are rather amusing: "En "votre qualité d' Européen, ne considérez "pas la flatterie comme un moyen que "vous ne puissiez employer; elle est très-"ordinaire parmi les nations Asiatiques, et "quoiqu'il puisse vous en coûter, il vous "sera très-avantageux de ne pas craindre "de la prodiguer." I should say, with all deference, that flattery will not go far amongst orientals, unless interest has been made apparent, or fear and respect have been first inspired, and that an open straight-forward mode of dealing is generally the best, as being a system of conduct likely, on account of its rarity amongst themselves, to excite attention and command success.

It is, however, to the masterly and recently published work of M. Levchine, that we are indebted for a large and most interesting mass of information respecting the Kirghiz-Kazaks, who inhabit the northern part of those regions that have the sea of Aral as their centre, part of which is now the theatre of the Russian invasion of Khiva. It is seen, that the banks of the sea of Aral have been accurately surveyed by Russian engineers, who have been occupied in the steppes, or plains, of the Kirghiz-Kazaks, from the years 1820 to 1826, that its level is much higher (one hundred and eighteen feet ?) than that of the Caspian, and that the natives say there is a whirlpool in the centre, which no vessel can approach with safety ; a circumstance, if true, which would lead us to suspect the existence of a subterranean communication with the Caspian. We learn also, that the Kirghiz-Kazaks inhabit an immense extent of country, lying between forty-two and fifty-five degrees north latitude, and extended from sixty-eight degrees thirty-five minutes, to one hundred and two degrees east longitude, from Ferro. That it is bounded on the north and west by the mountains of Siberia, the river Ural, and part of the Caspian sea, and that the eastern frontier is bounded by the chain of Chinese fortresses; whilst on the south the Kirghiz-Kazaks are met by the Turkomans, who rove on the eastern bank of the Caspian, and the same frontier continued to the eastward, adjoins that of Tashkhend, that of the Turkistanis, and the countries occupied by the Buruts, or Kirghiz. These last (who also inhabit the plains of Pamere, and plunder the caravans passing between Ladak and Yarkund) are quite a distinct race from the Kirghiz-Kazaks, formerly the subjects of Arslan Khan, Alp Arslan, the cotemporary of the Emperor Baber, who could bring four hundred thousand of them into the field. They are now divided into three distinct hordes, the great, the middle, and the little, whose united population amounts to upwards of four millions. We find that the cause of this division originally, was, according to their traditions, a partition of the country amongst the three sons of one of their deceased Khans. The Little Horde is the nearest to Europe; its winter quarters are always upon the banks of the Syr, or Jaxartes; upon which river M. Levchine has furnished us with a very learned dissertation. This river enters the sea of Aral. The horde is also at the mouth of the Emba, which empties itself into the Caspian. In summer, the horde remains upon the banks of the Emba. The Middle Horde occupies an extent of country which lies more to the eastward. The Great Horde extends itself to the frontiers of China. A few of the Kirghiz-Kazaks are to be found at Khiva, but the inhabitants of Khiva are Usbeks and Turkomans. The true Tartar is the native of Kasan. M. Levchine gives a history of the manner in which the Kirghiz-Kazaks have gradually become the subjects of Russia; and adds the following remarks, which apply equally to the Turkomans of the desert. "No zealous Mahometan regards as sacred, a convention made with a Christian. The Kirghiz respects the obligations by which his forefathers have bound him so much the less, because he is persuaded that they could never bind any but themselves, and that for the son and grandson there is no other law but personal advantage, &c." M. Levchine says, that, as from the nature of the soil he inhabits, the Kirghiz can never be an agriculturist, he procures grain from his neighbours in exchange for cattle. It is more than ninety years since the Kirghiz have been considered as being under the dominion of Russia; and eighty years have elapsed since the Russian Government has in vain exerted itself to establish amongst them a certain organization; but that money expended, trouble taken, and advice given, have all been hitherto without effect; whilst the repeated attacks of the Kirghiz upon the Russian lines, the carrying off horses and those whom they take prisoners, the pillage of the caravans, their frequent actions with Russian detachments, and numerous acts of violence of the same nature, enable us to see what idea the Kirghiz have of their subjection to Russia.

M. Levchine informs us that the climate of the Kirghiz Kazaks is particularly remarkable for the extremes of heat and cold; the winters are very rigorous, the heat of the dog-days insupportable. The cold, in some part of the Steppes, and near the embouchure of the river Syr or

Jaxartes in latitude forty-five degrees, descends to twenty and thirty degrees of Reaumur; and, in the countries near the river Ural, which are much more to the north, the heat amounts to fifty degrees of Reaumur in the sun, and to thirty-four in the shade. The soldiers of Timour Lung died of the cold on the banks of the Syr. M. Levchine remarks of the climate of the Steppes in general, that the spring appears suddenly, and passes away rapidly; that the summer is dry and burning; that the autumn is rainy, gloomy, and short; that the winter is long, dry, and constantly cold. The Kirghiz, he adds, rarely encamp in a large number at the same spot, as there would not be sufficient space for their cattle; while the Steppes of the Kirghiz Kazaks are without water, whence results an excessive dryness, which is to be attributed to the scarcity of rain and the extreme heat of summer; that salt is found every where, and that waters free from salt are very rare. The soil of the Steppes is of clay, or clay mixed with sand, and almost always impregnated with salt; and, in many places, the aspect of the country offers to the sight evident traces of having been, as it were, recently covered by the waves of the sea. The enormous snows of winter, when melted, produce water which ought to compensate for the want of rain; but it cannot sink deeply into the clay soil, in consequence of the opposition offered by the substratum of rock which lies under it; so that the waters of the melted snows run in great masses, precipitating themselves towards the rivers, lakes, morasses, and moving sands, without having time to dilute the large spaces which they traverse in this furious manner. Scarped banks and deep ravines are thus produced, and large crevices are formed by the heat of the sun;

and the same substratum of rock is probably also the obstacle which is opposed to the formation of fresh springs. In his chapter on the mountains found in the centre of the plains of the Kirghiz Kazaks, M. Levchine has given us a curious remark of M. Changine, on the Mount Iman, situated near the lake of that name, on the right bank of the Ichim. "The mountains are of granite; but they astonish the geologist, and arrest the attention of the observer, in that they are divided, throughout the whole length of their horizontal development from north to south, by parallel beds of quartz and siliceous slate. These beds have the appearance of remains of walls, from two to six sagénes, (each about six feet seven inches in thickness,) and elevate themselves above the superficies of the mountains from fourteen to sixteen inches. The granite which separates them is from fifty to one hundred sagenes thick.

I here propose a just observation: a phenomenon so new contradicts the theories of the formation of primitive substances, and makes me abstain from all conclusion."

The land of the Kirghiz Kazaks most free from sand, and most fertile, is in their northern region, between fifty-one and fifty-five degrees of latitude. Its extremity may be figured in idea by a line, which would be extended between the fortress of Orsk and the foot of Semiarsk; possessing on the eastern side of it the qualifications necessary for colonization, abounding in pasture, wood, and water.

The isthmus which separates the Caspian from the sea of Aral is called by the Kirghiz Kazaks the Oust-Ourt, signifying, in their own language, a "plateau, or high plain." Its narrowest width does not appear to exceed one hundred and sixty-five miles. The length of the sea of Aral is about two hundred and seventy miles, and its breadth one hundred and forty. The Oust-Ourt, says M. Levchine, is not watered by a single river; and it no where produces good forage, or means of subsistence [denrées]. The briars and herbage which grow there are good for camels, but not for horses, still less for sheep. Springs are rare, and the water is far from the surface of the earth. Winds and hurricanes are added to the infertility of the soil, so that the elevated and exposed plains are entirely uninhabited, and the Kirghiz Kazaks have never encamped there in winter. M. Levchine inserts a geological account of the Oust-Ourt, extracted from the journal of M. Eversmaun, naturalist to a Russian expedition under Major General Berg, which was sent, in 1825-6, to make a description of it. Amongst other remarks he informs us, that the height of the plateau, above the sea of Aral, no where exceeds six hundred feet.

He has given us a valuable account of the different routes by which these regions are traversed, from north to south. By one of the two first which he mentions the Russians most probably marched towards Khiva. They lead from the fortress of Saraïtchi. Kovskaia, across the Emba river, on the north of the Caspian, to Khiva, by the Oust-Ourt; after having descended from which, all the caravans move forward to Khiva, where they arrive in twenty-five or twenty-six days' march. The ruins of buildings, the remains of fortifications, and some solidly-constructed wells, show that these two routes were opened by people anterior to the Kirghiz Kazaks, and are by some attributed to the descendants of Chenghiz Khan. Another route, longer than the former, but more convenient, passes over the Oust-Ourt, and then follows the banks of the Sea of Aral downwards to the Oxus.

There are many routes from Orenburg to Bokhara. The most remarkable is that followed by the Russian mission under Baron Meyendorf, in 1820, which is detailed, and occupied from the tenth of October to the twentieth of December.

There are two routes from Orenburg direct to Khiva, without passing by the fort of Saraitchi Kovskaia. One, which follows the route to Bokhara, joining the north-east bank of the Sea of Aral, and following it downwards to Hurghunge. The second running along the western bank of the Sea of Aral. Orsk [Yeman-Kala] is the point in the Russian frontier which is nearest to Bokhara. Many routes for Bokhara commence at Orsk, which are reunited as they approach the Syr, or Jaxartes. In 1821, Baron Meyendorf returned from Bokhara to Orsk, and estimated the distance between the two places from one thousand two hundred and fifty to one thousand three hundred versts; somewhat less than one thousand English miles, a verst being three quarters of a mile. The latitude of Khiva is forty-one degrees, forty minutes; and its longitude seventy-eight degrees, ten minutes, from the Isle of Ferro. The latitude of Orenburg is fifty-one degrees, forty minutes; its longitude seventy-two degrees, fifty minutes, from the Isle of Ferro. Orsk appears to be about twenty-five miles to the southward of Orenburg, and about one hundred and ninety miles to the east of it.

M. Levchine mentions several other routes, from Troitska to Bokhara, and from the fortress of Petropaulovskaia to Bokhara.

From Semiarsk to Tashkhend.

Another route to the same place, and another from the fortress of Bouhtarminskaia to the Chinese frontier at Tchougoutchaka, occupies twenty-three days in the middle of summer.

Also another, by the same traveller, M. Poutimtzof, on his return, of four hundred and fifty-eight versts, whilst his former journey was of four hundred and six versts.

Also another, by Sub-Ensign Teliatniskof, from the fort of Koriakovsky to the town of Turkistan, which occupied twenty-nine days, being one thousand one hundred and sixty versts; on the supposition that he travelled forty versts a-day.

M. Levchine finishes his remarks on the routes by saying, that the spring, and particularly the month of May, is the best season for travelling in the plains of the Kirghiz Kazaks; it being the time when the herbs are fresh and abundant, the waters are not yet dried up, and the heat is still supportable.

The chapter on the commerce carried on by the Kirghiz Kazaks with the neighbouring countries appears to me so interesting and valuable, that I have here translated nearly the whole of it, and almost literally. M. Levchine says, "Frequent as the attacks, accompanied by pillage and devastation, of the Kirghiz Kazaks may be upon the countries contiguous to their Steppes, commerce is a recompense for all the losses caused by their foolish and impudent rapacity; commerce, we say, renders their vicinity very advantageous to China, but still much more so to Russia.

The Khivians, the Bokharis, the inhabitants of Tachkhend and Kohen, as well as those of Little Bokhara and Oriental Turkistan, trade with them; but with less advantage than the Russians and Chinese, for these reasons:—

"First, That there are a great quantity of manufactured goods delivered by China and Russia to the hordes of the Kirghiz, of such a nature, that a great part of them would not find an outlet elsewhere.

"Secondly, The need that China and Russia have of raw produce, which they receive from the Kirghiz, at a low price, in exchange for manufactured goods.

"Thirdly, The measures taken by the Governments of both empires for the extension of commerce. However, the measures taken are not at all the same on the part of the two states. The Russian Government, to arrive at its end, employs expense and care; forms establishments, and establishes markets of exchange; gives to the Kirghiz privileges, arms the caravans, distributes presents. The Chinese employ menace, vexations, and a despotic severity. They themselves set a value upon the cattle which are brought to them; give in exchange merchandize, or ingots [sycee] of silver, according to their own regulations, and sometimes according to their own good pleasure; and, in order to avoid disputes, complaints, explanations, questions, and exactions [avanies], with the Chinese Government, the Kazaks return murmuring, the Chinese forbidding them to enter their towns. With regard to this note I may be allowed to remark here, that those whom I have questioned in Tibet and Kashmir, on the subject of the Chinese Government of

Yarkund, speak in the highest terms of its justice generally.

"Fourthly, The great number of people who partake of these advantages; and, finally, for the advantage, in particular, of Russia, we have,

"Fifthly, The immense extent over which this commerce takes place, enriching the inhabitants of the lines [lignes] of Orenburg and Siberia.

"The Kirghiz are, with regard to the Russians, for all transactions of their commerce, in the situation of the Russians with regard to the French and English in their relations with them. The commerce of the Kirghiz is carried on by exchange. Accustomed to sell and buy in this manner, the Kirghiz in general care not to know the value of monies: fearing always to be deceived in receiving money, they always demand the most exorbitant sums for objects of the least value, or absolutely reject every bargain, where a question of money arises. Orenburg, Troitsk, the forts Petropavlofsk Presnogorkofskoi, Ormsk (Yeman Kala), Semipalatinsk, Oust-Kamenogorskaia, and Ouralsk, are the places where they come to trade in the greatest numbers. Orenburg is the most important of all. The Kirghiz trade principally with the Chinese at Kovldja, or, as the Chinese call it, Ili.

The best time for commerce or exchange is from the middle of June to the middle of November. The Kirghiz go for the purpose of making exchanges to Khiva, Bokhara, Kokan, and Tashkhend, whither also other trading people go. The inhabitants of these last cities themselves sometimes transport their merchandise into the Kirghiz villages, or exchange a part of it when they traverse the Steppes to come to Russia; but the Russians and Chinese only trade with them upon their respective frontiers. The merchandise which the Kirghiz deliver to their neighbours is the same every where. It can assuredly only consist of their flocks, or the produce of their flocks. In detail, it comprises sheep, horses, horned cattle, camels, goats, goats' hair, wool of different animals and of different qualities; skins of goats, foxes, korsaks (?), hares and marmots, felts, armiatchina (?), dakhi (a kind of habit), touloupes (sheep-skins sewn together in pelisses), horns of antelopes, and madder roots. These are the articles which the Kirghiz hordes furnish to Russia and other nations, but the Russians have the greater share of them.

M. Levchine speaks of the great quantity of money which the Kirghiz, the Bokharis, and the Khivians, possessed from 1748 to 1755. It formed part of the pillaged treasure, after the death of Nadir Shah; and these three last-mentioned people came to the Russian frontiers with bags full of Indian rupees, and other oriental coins, or with ingots of precious metal.

He gives a table, containing a detailed account of the number of horses, oxen, sheep, and goats, that have been exchanged in commerce by the Kirghiz, at Orenburg, from the year 1745 to 1820. Before the year 1745, the Kirghiz were not known at Orenburg, except by their incursions.

In 1745, the number exchanged was as follows:—

Horses and colts five hundred and fifty-two; oxen two; sheep three thousand and fifty-three; goats fifty-two.

In 1820, horses and colts sixty-eight; oxen one thousand and seventy-four; sheep one hundred and sixty-thousand two hundred and ninety-six; goats three thousand two hundred and sixty-eight.

The old inhabitants of Orenburg say, that in 1786-7, the commerce was most flourishing, and affirm at that place alone six hundred thousand sheep were exchanged by the Kirghiz. Including other places, probably not less than a million of sheep crossed the Russian frontier in each of these years.

The number of horses that entered by Orenburg and different places, amounted to fifty thousand a year: now, on the contrary, the Kirghiz buy the Russian horses in great numbers.

The Kirghiz do not exchange many camels with the Russians, but the Khivians and the Bokharis buy a great number. The commerce of the Kirghiz in great cattle is very inconsiderable, and almost entirely carried on at Troïtsk. The Kirghiz say, that they used to deliver to their neighbours in China, Bokhara, Khiva, and different countries, as much cattle as they exchanged away to Russia, altogether amounting to two million sheep, and one hundred thousand horses, without speaking of other merchandise. M. Levchine proceeds to remark, that this state of things was very probable during the last century, but is impossible under existing circumstances; and that internal dissensions and Barantas (incursions for mutual reprisal, made by one horde into the settlements of another) have so diminished the number of their flocks, and the Khirghiz studs, that they do not send above half the quantity of cattle they sent formerly; and that in the first years of this century, the exchange of the Russians with the Kirghiz was in a still more wretched state.

In 1820, the whole number of cattle of all kinds exchanged along the frontier, did not exceed four hundred and eleven thousand.

We may infer, from all this, that the Russian population, and their breed of horses, is fast increasing; and that their farms are in such a thriving state, that they have far less occasion than formerly to seek assistance from their neighbours.

The Kirghiz take in return for their cattle, and the raw produce which they import into Russia, various articles in cast iron and copper, such as cauldrons, tripods on which they place them, sewing thimbles, needles, scissars, knives, hatchets, padlocks, scythes, sickles, &c.; also woollen cloths, velvets, brocades, silk stuffs, lace, ribands, handkerchiefs, cords, boxes, alum, copperas, false pearls, little glasses, linen, snuff, white and red paint, beaver skins, and worked leather called couftes. This leather is known in Kashmir, and the northern parts of India, as "Bolgar," and is that which we know in Europe as Russian leather; and is called Bolgar, from the ancient kingdom of Bolgaria, which formerly flourished on the banks of the Volga, in the countries which now form the government of Kasan and Simbirsk; whence Central Asia was furnished with all the productions of the north.

If we reflect on the immense advantages which the Russian government gains from this commerce, we shall perceive that it has no cause to regret the expenses it incurs, on account of the appointment of Khans and elders, for the presents which it heaps upon them, and even for the maintenance of officers charged with the management of the hordes. The troops appointed to protect the frontiers, are not included in this remark, for the government maintained them at a period when, in fact, no commerce existed between the Kirghiz and the Russians.

The Chinese principally furnish to the Kirghiz, silken stuffs, porcelain, brocades, silver, tea, glazed pottery, and the other produce of their manufactories.

The Bokharis, the Khivians, and the inhabitants of Tachkhend, furnish them with silk and cotton stuffs, quilted robes, fusils, sabres, and powder. In exchange, independently of the produce of the flocks, the hordes furnish slaves, carried off from the Russian frontiers.

In speaking of the commerce of the Kirghiz, we should not neglect to note that they act as agents for the trade of Russia with Central Asia. This interposition is injurious, and always dangerous, but the merchants of Khiva, Bokhara, Kashkar, Tachkhend, and the neighbouring cities, are of necessity obliged to have recourse to them, not being able to gain the Russian frontiers, nor to return home, but by crossing the Kirghiz Steppes; where the traveller, without guide and defence, is continually exposed to the danger of being pillaged and assassinated, or of dying from thirst. Moreover, the Kirghiz, besides being employed as defenders and guides (Karekachs), voluntarily take upon themselves to transport merchandise upon their own camels.

Before the submission of the Kirghiz to Russia, or rather before the establishment of the line of Orenburg, the Bokharis and Khivians usually traded to Astrakan, where they arrived by sea, on the eastern shore of the Caspian, chiefly from Manghichlak, where they left their camels. Besides, the Bokharis sometimes sent their caravans even into Siberia. Siberia, I may here remark, signifies the east, sun-rise, or day-break; and the word sibiri in the east is used with either of these meanings.

At first sight, it seems that this last circumstance ought to facilitate commerce, and benefit the people who receive the price of these transports; and, much more the merchants who, without it, would find themselves obliged to traverse immense deserts upon their own camels, and would meet upon their way numerous and formidable obstacles; but a further examination shows us, that the assistance of the Kirghiz is, for the merchants of High Asia, a source still more productive of difficulties, obstacles, and losses.

In 1820, and the two following years, the Kirghiz charged eighty or one hundred rubles (ten-pence each) for a camel going from Orenburg to Bokhara; and from fifty-five to eighty, from Orenburg to Khiva.

The first difficulties for the merchants, after having made their bargain and commenced their journey, arise from their having no right to regulate the march of the caravan, nor to meddle with the measures or dispositions. Of these, whatever they may be, the conductors now become absolute masters. The Kirghiz choose the direction of the route, regulate the days for halting, the encampment for the night, the moments of repose, and obey none but the caravan-bashee, or chief, who himself sometimes meets with resistance and contradiction from them. Thinking much less of the means for shortening the journey than of their own business, they usually try to conduct the caravan by their settlements, where they can, without expense, lay in a fresh stock of provisions: there they repose for some days, and in case of need, change such of their camels as are fatigued, or on whose service they cannot reckon. This custom has determined certain directions for the routes, and has given them different names: one is called the Tchoumakeï, because it passes through the districts of that tribe.

The indispensable necessity of following the routes which the guides thus choose, and the loss of time during the journey, are still nothing compared to the risks to which the merchants in the Steppes are exposed. There they are stopped by some formidable chief, who makes an arbitrary demand for their right of way across his pasturage; and he menaces them, in case of refusal, with the retention of all their goods. Further on, they meet a chief who summons them, and threatens them: elsewhere they find a troop of armed brigands, who, either through a feud with the guides, or urged by the love of plunder, make a sudden attack, and conduct themselves with the greatest ferocity.

The less powerful tribes hardly ever trust themselves with the escort of the caravans; and the protection of those which are more formidable is only useful when there are no serious dissensions between them and any other; there is no safety else for commerce. The caravans, in case of discord and revenge, being considered as the property of the guides, fall victims to the hatred which is borne to them, or to the reprisals which are to be made from them. The Russian governor of Orenburg, Neplovief, demanded of a chief the reason for pillaging a caravan. He replied, that he did so because it passed not through his settlements, but those of his enemy.

M. Levchine finishes by remarking, that Russia has employed many and mild means for the purpose of putting an end to these violences and brigandages; but all have remained ineffectual; and experience has shown, that whilst the Kirghiz keep their rapacious inclinations, and are not restrained by force (à main armée), the commerce of the Russians with Central

Asia cannot prosper. This truth is the fruit of a hundred years of experience and observation.

The Russian Government, conformably to the conclusion of M. Levchine, has put the caravans destined to traverse the Steppes of the Kirghiz Kazaks under the protection of a well-armed escort. Russian commerce may promise itself the greatest advantages from this measure.

After the details which are here epitomized, I think, with all deference, that M. Levchine should rather have spoken of the immense advantages that have accrued to Russia from the commerce that has been, or of that which may accrue from henceforth, that is, if Khiva be subdued; because, as the number of cattle that cross into the frontiers of Siberia has been decreasing, and the number of horses that cross from thence has been increasing, it would appear, as I have already remarked, that the Russians have enough of their own; and the Kirghiz commerce being that of exchange, it is obvious that the consumption of manufactured goods, from the time present, will diminish in proportion.

It is probable that Russia has long entertained the idea of invading the Oasis of Khiva; and, speaking independently of their motives for undertaking the expedition, that the present force has been marched at this juncture in order to counterbalance the check which her diplomacy has so lately received in Afghanistan, and of maintaining an imposing position in the eyes of the inhabitants of Asia. We learn from M. Levchine, that Russia has long been in possession of most accurate information regarding the countries of which he treats, of the routes through them, and of their geography, geology, climate, soil, productions, and capabilities. But we may fairly suppose, that no Russian, or other conseiller d'état, can publish all he knows; and, therefore, largely as we are indebted to M. Levchine, it is probable that he has kept back a great deal of valuable political information, for which we have no right to inquire. At the same time, so interesting are his materials, so masterly and comprehensive his arrangement, and so opportune the time of publication, that we run considerable risk of being allured into the belief, that Russia, by invading Khiva, has no ulterior views beyond the extension of her commerce, or the manumission of her enslaved subjects. Besides, what rational being will venture to say that Russia has no right to march for the united purposes of securing to herself an advanced depôt, whence she can radiate her commerce to every part of Central Asia, and of releasing many thousands of her own subjects from a miserable captivity? Although it may be remarked, that, with twenty-three million of serfs, she might as well have commenced the work of liberation a little nearer home.

From all the accounts, then, that we can collect of these countries, we may fairly infer, that a Russian army has no ordinary difficulties to contend with, in attempting to cross the Steppes of Central Asia. Every precaution has, of course, been taken that could contribute to her success; and a communication, for the purposes of co-operation and assistance, will, no doubt, be kept up with the shores of the Caspian. But I can never be persuaded, as some accounts have it, that any of the wild children of the desert, either Kirghiz or Turkomans, can be friendly to the advance of the Russians. I should think it most likely that their feuds will be set aside, and that, assisted and stimulated by the Bokharis, they will unite as in a common cause against a common invader. There are no Mussulmen so strict as the inhabitants of Bokhara, and none who would fight so desperately in defence of their religion. Sir Alexander Burnes has called it the centre of Islam, and says that they have twenty thousand cavalry. I have heard from the natives themselves that their force is much larger. The Turkoman is not so zealous in his faith; but, being a Suni Mahomedan, finds it convenient to have a religious feud with the Persians, who are Shiahs, because it yields him a pretext for carrying off, enslaving, and converting them. The Kirghiz, who have but a confused idea of the religion of the Prophet, might gladly avail themselves of a similar pretext; and, at the united instigation of the Bokharis and the Turkomans, and the still more powerful exhortations of their own sorcerers, or Baksy, (those of the grand horde of the Kirghiz ride on white horses, and gallop over the plains like persons possessed,) would combine in a religious war against the Infidels. The love of plunder alone would excite them to attack, as the Kirghiz display an avarice and cupidity which is quite extraordinary. Their prisoners say, that they have seen them tear the smallest trifle in pieces; and that their ignorance and determination to have a share is so inflexible, that if they got possession of a watch, they would break it up, and one would carry off a wheel, another a screw, another a hand, and another a spring.

The horses of the Kirghiz Kazaks are trained to run races, in distances sometimes from twenty-five and thirty to forty and fifty versts; and are often ridden so hard, that they fall dead at the end of the course. Sir John Mc Neill once told me, in Persia, an anecdote related amongst the Turkomans, which is very characteristic. The owner of a very superior young horse saw a man in the act of galloping off with him. He immediately gave chase, but was surprised at his nearing him, because he knew that the horse he rode himself was far inferior in speed. He observed, however, that his favourite animal was impeded by his trappings; and, sooner than see him beaten, even under such circumstances, the owner, acting on the impulse of the moment, called out to the robber, and told him he was a fool for not cutting the particular rope that hampered him!

The Kirghiz have another kind of race, in which the men dispute, in address and agility, with young females. A couple start off on horseback, and the cavalier, when he has caught up her who races with him, is bound to cross her in the course, or to touch her bosom with his hand. However gross may be the manners of the Kirghiz beauties, they will only allow this liberty to those whom they like; they otherwise contrive to keep their partner at a distance, by their quickness in turning, or blows of the whip if necessary. The best Kirghiz horses are always used for battle.

Space is measured in the Steppes by time, by the sight and the hearing. When they wish to speak of a great extent they talk of so many days; and what part of a day it occupies to accomplish it on horseback, or on a camel. In order to determine the distance of an approached place, they take, as a measure, the maximum of the space over which they can hear the cry of a man, or of that to which the sight can carry. The goodness of their sight is admirable; they distinguish in the plain little objects at the distance of ten versts (seven and a half miles) or more; and where an European, with good eyes, would only distinguish mere points, the Kirghiz recognize the form and colour of objects.

Every Kirghiz, in setting out on a journey, fastens to his saddle a bag of kroute, a cheese made from sour milk. He soaks some of it in water, and thus appeases his hunger and thirst together. When going against an enemy he sews behind him, on his outer garment, one or two little bags, containing written prayers, which are supposed to give him courage, and preserve him from illness and wounds.

The Kirghiz Kazaks fight with the lance, the sabre, arrows, the matchlock, and the tchakane, a kind of hatchet; and, for defensive armour, wear a coat of mail, and sometimes a helmet. The powder they make is very bad, as they are ignorant of the proportions of its ingredients. They also make a kind which is white.

A Kirghiz, says M. Levchine, remains easily a whole day without drinking, and two without eating; so that, upon the first opportunity, he eats enormously. As a proof of his strength of body, he adds, that a Kirghiz ties a sheep to his saddle, and gallops between two rows of spectators. Those who wish to try their strength ought to tear off the legs of the wretched animal, whilst he is thus dragged along at full speed.

The Kirghiz does not fight for war, but for pillage; and, therefore, a compact front or square of good infantry will resist a mass of Kirghiz ten times more numerous. A single piece of cannon will destroy an incredible number of them. Trembling with fear at the sight of a gun, they collect themselves in face of the muzzle, trying to hide one behind the other, and the ball pierces a long file of them. A caravan, which was pillaged as it was going to Bokhara, defended itself a long time against these bandits by means of the funnel or pipe of the Russian copper kettle, placed upon a camel, which the aggressors took for a small cannon, or falconet. They took flight two or three times, perceiving that a cunning fellow was pointing the pipe towards them. What ravage would not a single company of European artillery commit amongst this ignorant people!

Their incursions are generally made without order, by night, and unawares; but they are executed with incredible rapidity, with loud cries, and with different arms, sabres, matchlocks, bows and arrows, sticks, stones, and arkanes, or long cords terminated by a running knot. Their first attack is always vigorous, and almost irresistible. They then display all their valour; but, in case of non-success, they lose it as soon, and gain the open plain with the greatest cowardice. If they are dismounted, and obliged to fight on foot, it is all up with them. Sometimes, nevertheless, they do a great deal of harm to the bravest adversaries, by carrying off their horses upon the slightest negligence, by cutting off their convoys in case of a division of forces, and, if they can, by making prisoners of the sentinels of the advanced posts, by means of their arkanes or cords. The same kind of attack is carried on by the formidable Moguls, the Bedouins, the Kurds, the Turkomans, and other people who resemble the Kirghiz Kazaks.

I think we may expect to hear that the Russians have met with numerous difficulties, have undergone many privations and fatigues, arising from natural obstacles alone, and have sustained considerable loss of baggage, camels, cattle, and camp equipage, either by abandonment or foray: that they are kept in a constant state of watchfulness and excitement, by the harassing and nightly attacks and demonstrations of the Turkomans, who are a far more formidable enemy than the Kirghiz; and that their own Cossack troops, whom they will doubtless oppose to them, will not be able to meet them on equal terms; the deserts being at once their home, their shelter, and a fortress from which they cannot be expelled. Lieut. Conolly has remarked, that the Russians seem to have established a good understanding with the Turkomans settled along the eastern coast of the Caspian. I would venture to doubt its continuance in case of invasion, however advantageous it may be to the latter for the purposes of trade.

The latest accounts inform us of the halt of General Berowski, (the General Berowski, a son of Prince Radzivill, who was well known in Persia, was killed at Herat,) on the banks of the Emba, in consequence of the quantity of snow in his front. M. Levchine, however, speaking of the plains which extend towards the Oust-Ourt, after adverting to their complete sterility, remarks, that in summer and autumn there is no place more disadvantageous, even for Nomade tribes; but that in winter, the Kirghiz find there many conveniences; and that the rushy places, which cover the plain like forests, serve first, as a rampart against winds and hurricanes (bouranes): secondly, as pasturage for cattle: thirdly, instead of firewood. The Russians have thus probably been stopped by a winter of unusual severity. M. Levchine adds, that the Oust-Ourt is remarkable for the rigour of its climate; that thirty degrees of Reaumur appear nothing extraordinary; and that the snow lies there from two to three feet in thickness.

However desirable may be the approach of spring, it is far from being without its disadvantages as a season for marching. Immediately upon the melting of the snows, the paths are crossed by resistless torrents, and the numerous ravines are turned into water-courses.

Lieut. Conolly has remarked, vol. i. p. 144, the "Caspian desert is generally of a light soil, white and inclined to be sandy, yet so firm, that in dry weather camels barely leave the print of their feet upon it."

A dry sand affords a secure footing to a camel, but that animal, when laden, walks so insecurely upon a moistened and slippery soil, (to say nothing of the additional fatigue in consequence of forced marches,) that he is always in danger of falling, even upon level ground; and the injury he often receives is of such a nature, that it is charity to put him to death. To the spring, which appears suddenly, and passes away rapidly, succeeds a dry and burning summer.

The Russian force from Mangichlak and Orenburg has been estimated, I know not with what accuracy, at thirty-two thousand men. The distance, by M. Levchine's map, from Mangichlak on the Caspian to Urghunj, in a straight line, is four hundred miles, to Khiva four hundred and sixty miles.

From the embouchure of the Emba, where the Russians are said to have halted, to Urghunj, in a straight line, is four hundred and thirteen miles, and to Khiva five hundred and five miles. The forced marches of a caravan from one watering-place to another, are thirty, forty, or fifty miles. I have marched forty-eight in one night, in Persia. Those of an army would, I suppose, be much less.

The inhabitants of Khiva, including the Turkomans, are estimated by M. Moravief, as already noticed, at three hundred thousand; of these, thirty thousand are Usbeks, lords of the soil by right and conquest. One hundred thousand are Sâts, the inhabitants of the country before the Usbeks took it. The Kara Kalpaks, south of lake Aral, are as many; and the remainder are Turkomans, a few Kirghiz, and Tajiks.

Facts thus detailed and brought forward, as a foundation for conjecture, should not fairly be supposed to comprise either prophecy or assertion; but I cannot help thinking, that the success of the Russians, in their invasion of Khiva, is rather problematical than otherwise, that is, supposing its achievement be attempted in one campaign.

The French expeditions in Africa, are in many respects similar to that of the Russians in Asia.

But let us suppose the desert and the protecting distance to be passed, the difficulties that were looked upon as insurmountable to have been conquered, the Russians in possession of Khiva, the Russian artillery "en potence" upon the western bank of the Oxus, and awaiting but the orders of the Emperor to be transported on its stream, to within a short distance of Bokhara. The navigation of the river thus commanded, and the humbled Moslems may find it convenient to liberate their Russian slaves by way of propitiation, and afterwards to agree to any terms that the invader may dictate.

But the motives of Russia, as detailed in the manifesto, are "to put an end to robbery and exaction, and to deliver those Russians who are detained in slavery; to make the inhabitants of Khiva respect and esteem the Russian name; and finally to strengthen in that part of Asia the lawful influence to which Russia has a right, and which alone can ensure the maintenance of peace. This is the purpose of the present expedition; and as soon as it shall be attained, and an order of things conformable to the interests of Russia and the neighbouring Asiatic states shall be established on a permanent footing, the body of troops that has received orders to march on Khiva, will return to the frontiers of the empire." It remains to be seen, whether Russia will content herself with having rendered a service to civilization by the chastisement of the Khivians, or whether she will not show herself ambitious of further acquisition.

Supposing, that at any future period she should march upon Bokhara, she would, I think, meet with a desperate resistance, ere she could enter the holy city; but there is no doubt, that with a large force, properly organized at Khiva, she could soon make herself mistress of it. But as, according to her manifesto, its conquest is not her immediate object, she will, nevertheless, find herself in a position to increase her influence as much as she pleases. Persia, at least, is fond of the British alliance, and if left to herself, would not long hesitate as to which should be her friend.

Riding once at Tehran with Sir John Campbell and the British mission, to dine with Count Simonitch, the Russian Ambassador, I remember that a well-dressed Persian in the crowd called out, that one hair of that Ambassador's head was worth an hundred of the other's; and I believe that he spoke the sentiments of the many. But Persia is already too much be-Russianized, and will now, moreover, feel really grateful to Russia for her chastisement of her enemies, the Khivians, and disposed perhaps to grant her some additional boon: the bazaars of every city, north of the Hindu Kosh, will be flooded more than ever, with Russian manufactures: the interests of the Uzbegs of Kunduz, the Bokharis, the Kokanis, (said to be nearly, if not quite, as powerful as the Bokharis,) and those of the Chinese in Yarkund, who, as I have been informed, are constantly quarrelling, if not at open war, with the

Kokanis, can be played off against each other. Shah Shuja can be tampered with; Kamran of Herat can be intrigued with, and Dost Mohamed Khan can be encouraged at the same moment.

When the Russians at any future time have established themselves at Bokhara, it will become absolutely necessary that we should take possession of Kabul and Kandahar: and if we do not make ourselves masters of Herat, we should allow no foreign power to do so. It might be regarded as neutral ground.

But when the crisis has arrived, and the British and Russian frontiers are a limit to each other, let us not suppose,—as many do suppose,—that a sanguinary and nefarious contest must follow as a matter of course. When Russia, who knows we are not asleep, has made but a fair use of her local advantages, and, for the furtherance of apparently unexceptionable objects, has brought to reason the savage plunderers and bigots of the Asiatic deserts, — has inflicted upon them the penalty of adopting the semblance of humanity, and forced them to point out a safe path to the traveller,— let us try, without diminishing our watchfulness, to regard such movements with other feelings than those of jealousy and distrust; and to suppose that her ambition will not allow her to overstep the bounds of good policy and moderation, or suffer her to depreciate the merits of a success for which she would undoubtedly have the strongest claim upon the thanks of a civilized world.

It may be remarked, on the other hand, that England,—firm in purpose and determination, proud of her position in the East, obtained at the expense of a hundred victories, —will never seek further aggrandisement by grasping at more than is necessary for the preservation of what she has already acquired, and which she is so well able and knows so well how to defend.

Conquerors have advanced into distant regions and received the homage of nations previously unheard of; and, in most instances, their achievements have been accounted glorious, whether they have subdued for the love of conquest or the prospect of gain. Cortes and Pizarro were the successful invaders of the depths of a new world; and Cæsar led his legions into the untried wilds of Germany and Britain. Of Alexander it has been remarked by Bayle, that, "if books spoke the truth, he was the most extraordinary of all men; that he had nothing of mediocrity about him but his figure; that all the rest, good or bad, was in excess; that his ambition bordered upon madness; and that it was a crime to doubt the success of his designs;

that he was less a man than an incarnate intelligence; and that it might be said of him, that Providence had fixed upon him to evince to the earth the extent to which human forces may arrive, at a time when the most surprising revolutions happen." He marched from Europe, and gave audience to the ambassadors of Scythia and Palibothra. He would first have conquered, and then, after a fashion, would have civilized mankind. But never yet has it been known, that two great and Christianized nations, approaching from the east and from the west, have advanced their banners to its centre, from the demi-antipodal extremes of a mighty continent, to light up—or, if Providence so wills it, extinguish for ever—the signal-beacons of a desperate and universal war of opinion.

The first conference between the British and Russian commissioners, for the purpose of adjusting their mutual interests and lines of demarcation, will be fraught with results of the deepest importance to mankind. Few can be quite insensible to the glories of a victory, but all admit that triumph is dashed with misery; and battle, victory, and triumph, are common, and no novelties. The day that beholds such an event will mark the commencement of an era; and the page of history that relates it should be inscribed with newer and nobler characters than those of human blood. Let the good faith observable in the more honourable transactions of private life be introduced into those of a public nature, and we may soon hope to see the time when, by means of a chain of posts, steamboats, and railroads, (by which no fox-hunting will be spoiled), the overland journey, by way of St. Petersburgh or Warsaw, will become the quickest and most approved mode of travel between London and Calcutta.

BORDER ROUND MAHMUD'S TOMB.

APPENDIX.

" *Mahmud of Ghuzni marched thence across the desert; in his way to Guzerat and Somnath.*"—p. 25.

Rumzan, 415 ; October, 1024.

In the middle of the month of Rumzan, the Mohamedan army reached the city of Multan, and as a great desert lay before them, the king gave orders for the troops to provide themselves with several days' water and provisions, as also with provender for their horses, besides which, twenty thousand camels were laden with supplies. Having passed the desert, the army reached the city of Ajmeer. Here, finding the Rajah and inhabitants had abandoned the place, rather than submit to him, Mahmud ordered it to be sacked, and the adjacent country to be laid waste. Conceiving the reduction of the fort of Ajmeer would occupy too much time, he left it unmolested; and proceeding on his expedition, took by assault some smaller forts on the road, till at length he arrived at Nehrwala, a frontier city of Guzerat, which was evacuated on his approach. Mahmud, taking the same precautions as before, by rapid marches, reached Somnath without opposition. Here he saw a fortification on a narrow peninsula, washed on three sides by the sea, on the battlements of which appeared a vast host of people in arms, who, making a signal for a herald to approach, they proclaimed to him that their great idol, Somnath, had drawn the Mohamedans thither to blast them in a moment, and to revenge the destruction of the gods of India. In the morning, the Mohamedan troops advancing to the walls, began the assault. The battlements were in a short time cleared by the archers, and the Hindus, astonished and dispirited, crowded into the temple, and prostrating themselves in tears before the idol, prayed for assistance. The Mohamedans, having seized this opportunity, applied their scaling ladders and mounted the walls, shouting aloud, "Alla Akber[1]!" The Hindus, urged by despair, returned to the defence of the works, and made so spirited a resistance, that the Mohamedans, unable to retain their footing, and wearied with fatigue, fell back on all sides, and were at length obliged to retire. Next morning the action was renewed, but as fast as the besiegers scaled the walls, so fast were they hurled down headlong by the besieged, who now seemed resolved to defend the place to the last. Thus the labours of the second day proved even more unsuccessful than those of the first. On the third day, an army of idolaters having arrived to reinforce the garrison, presented itself in order of battle in sight of the Ghuzni camp. This manœuvre did not escape the king, who secured some boats left in a neighbouring creek, manned

[1] The war-cry of the Moslems, "God is Great!"

them with rowers and some of his best troops, and pursued the enemy; on which occasion, he took and sunk some of their flotilla, while a part only escaped. Having now placed guards round the walls and at the gates, Mahmud entered Somnath, accompanied by his sons and a few of his nobles, and principal attendants. On approaching the temple, he saw a superb edifice built of hewn-stone; its lofty roof was supported by fifty-six pillars curiously carved, and set with precious stones. In the centre of the hall was Somnath, a stone idol, five yards in height, two of which were sunk in the ground. The king, approaching the image, raised his mace and struck off its nose. He ordered two pieces of the idol to be broken off, and sent to Ghuzni, that one might be thrown at the threshold of the public mosque, and the other at the court door of his own palace. These identical fragments are to this day, (now six hundred years ago,) to be seen at Ghuzni. Two more fragments were reserved to be sent to Mecca and Medina. It is a well authenticated fact, that when Mahmud was thus employed in destroying this idol, a crowd of Brahmins petitioned his attendants, and offered a quantity of gold if the king would desist from further mutilation. His officers endeavoured to persuade him to accept of the money; for they said that breaking one idol would not do away with idolatry altogether; that, therefore, it could serve no purpose to destroy the image entirely; but that such a sum of money given in charity among true believers, would be a meritorious act. The king acknowledged there might be reason in what they said, but replied, that if he should consent to such a measure, his name would be handed down to posterity, as "Mahmud the idol seller," whereas he was desirous of being known as "Mahmud the destroyer:" he therefore directed the troops to proceed in their work. The next blow broke open the belly of Somnath, which was hollow, and discovered a quantity of diamonds, rubies, and pearls, of much greater value than the amount which the Brahmins had offered.

Mahmud determined to prevent this attempt to raise the siege, and having ordered a party to keep the garrison in check, himself engaged the enemy in the field. The battle raged with great fury: victory was long doubtful, till two Indian princes, Brahma Dew and Dabishleem, with other reinforcements, joined their countrymen during the action, and inspired them with fresh courage. Mahmud, at this moment perceiving his troops to waver, leaped from his horse, and prostrating himself before God[1], implored his assistance. Then mounting again, he took Abul Hussun, the Circassian, (one of his generals,) by the hand, by way of encouragement, and advanced on the enemy. At the same time, he cheered his troops with such energy, that, ashamed to abandon their king, with whom they had so often fought and bled, they, with one accord, gave a loud shout and rushed forwards. In this charge the Moslems broke through the enemy's lines, and laid five thousand Hindus dead at their feet. The rout became general. The garrison of Somnath, beholding this defeat, abandoned the defence of the place, and issuing out at a gate towards the sea, to the number of four thou-

[1] This mode of inspiring his troops, so often mentioned by the writers of the age, is extremely characteristic of the nature of the wars waged by Mahmud of Ghuzni in India.

sand, embarked in boats, intending to proceed to the island of Serendeep, or Ceylon.

"*The ruins of a large city called Zohaka.*"—p. 109.

Such was the information I received from the Lohanis. It was, perhaps, named after the Zohak of Ferdosi, a king of Persia, who dethroned and put to death Jemsheed, the founder of Persepolis.—Vide Sir John Malcolm's Persia, vol. i. p. 18.

"*The return of Alexander to a city he had founded amongst the Parapamisæ, is the best proof we have of his having originally crossed into Bactria, either by the pass of Bamian or that of the Hindu Kosh.*"—p. 196.

It is interesting to inquire into the reasons why Alexander, wishing to reach Bactria, did not march thither directly from Persia, without taking the trouble to go so far out of his way in order to cross by Bamian. But when he was on his way thither by the nearer road, he was suddenly recalled by the intelligence of a revolt at Artacæna, the capital city of Aria, which reached him at Susa. He then marched upon Artacæna, and this changed the whole plan of his campaign; for, instead of proceeding directly to Bactria, as he intended, he marched towards the countries of the Drangii and Arachosii, *i. e.* by the valley of the Helmund river, passing, no doubt, in the vicinity of the modern Kandahar. Sir John Mc Neill tells me, that the road by which he was probably marching, before his recal, is the open route from Herat to Balkh, by Meimuneh. It is possible, but highly improbable, that Alexander having once reached Kabul, should have arrived at Balkh by returning through the Hazara Jat mountains, from Kabul to Meimuneh.

That road has been passed by cavalry, and Baber relates, that he was nearly lost in the snow when crossing it. I think we may infer, altogether, that Alexander crossed at Bamian.

A Vocabulary from the language of that part of Kaffiristan which was known to my informant.—p. 238.

House, *amar*
Tree, *dogh*
Bread, *arve*
Water, *āb*
Wine, *chukera*
Meat, *undah*
Fowls, *ningatsah*
Dog, *soong*
Sword, *torauli*
Head, *shei*
Hair, *pasing*
Eye, *onche*
Eyebrow, *oncheshei*
Nose, *nos*
Mouth, *osh*
Teeth, *dont*
Ears, *khar*
Neck, *dameh*
Chest, *joh*
Stomach, *shon*
Shoulders, *unshei*
Hands, *dosh*
Feet, *khur (French pron.)*
Nails, *augl*
Bark, *onchun*
Knee, *zankhu*
Salaam, *purboyen*
Answer to salaam, *jya*
Wheat, *goum*
Flour, *brē*
Barley, *jau*
Bow, *shing drun*
Bow-string, *jhee*
Arrow, *khurn*
Hill, *dah*
Cow, *gau*
Goat, *wussi*
Sheep, *otini*
Ibex, *tsuve*
Morning, *evpei*
Noon, *ghurrish*
Afternoon, *evisa shei*
Evening, *tuttehvi shei*
Budh, *dghun*
Wild sheep, *godaur*
Wild deer, *murung*
Eagle, *koshi*
Sky, *kahl*
Sun, *maus*
Moon, *turrah*

1 Ev
2 Do
3 Drei
4 Chattah
5 Puch
6 Shu
7 Sop
8 Osht
9 No
10 Dosh
11 Yash
12 Bash
13 Trush
14 Chahardesh
15 Picheis
16 Sheizi
17 Saldosh
18 Oshtash
19 Kish
20 Bishei
30 Bishei dosh
40 Do ish
50 Do ish i dosh
60 Drei bish
70 Drei bish i dosh
80 Chattosh
90 Chattosh i dosh
100 Puch bish
200 Dosh bish

A thousand, he said, was 20×20.

THE END.